Touching Ground, Taking Root

Ed de la Torre

TOUCHING GROUND, TAKING ROOT

Theological and Political Reflections on the Philippine Struggle

in association with
the British Council of Churches

First published by
the Socio-Pastoral Institute, 530 Banawe St, Quezon City, Philippines.
This edition published by
the Catholic Institute for International Relations,
22 Coleman Fields, London N1 7AF,
in association with
the British Council of Churches, 2 Eaton Gate, London SW1

ISBN 0 946848 59 9

The British Council of Churches is sharing in the production of this book, but the opinion expressed is not necessarily that of the BCC Assembly.

Text and cover illustrations: Ed de la Torre
Cover Design: Eve White
Printed by the Russell Press Ltd, Gamble Street, Nottingham NG7 4ET

TABLE OF CONTENTS

DEDICATION

FOREWORD

Ed de la Torre usually signs his letters: 'In struggle and hope'. His life is a testimony to both: to the struggle against injustice and poverty in the Philippines, and the hope that its people will make their own history, and create a just society. This Christian commitment has led him to grapple with the major political issues of his day, has brought about his imprisonment for long years, and has given him the authority that stems from political commitment and sacrifice.

It is this authority that shines from his writings. But, more important, they reveal a depth of reflection that is the spiritual reward for active participation in the struggle for justice in the Philippines. The reflections in *Touching Ground, Taking Root* give us a unique insight into the choices faced by the church and popular organisations in the Philippines and many other parts of the Third World. In the sophistication of their political analysis they offer a model for those in the First World committed to the demands of the poor for justice, yet uncertain how to give practical support.

This alone would be justification for making Ed de la Torre's writings available to the widest possible public. But our link with him in Britain has historical roots also. Between his two spells in prison, he attended a 'Conference Towards a Theology for Britain in the '80s' and visited London. During the four years of his second prison term the British Council of Churches, Amnesty International and the United Nations Association issued an annual invitation to him, as a sign of protest, to preach at the Human Rights Day Service on 10 December.

Ed managed to keep up a correspondence from prison with friends in Britain, and CIIR and BCC staff attended his trial and were able to talk with him and his mother. The fall of the Marcos dictatorship resulted in his release and he has since played a critical role during the first months of the new government. In July 1986 he came to Britain again as the guest of CIIR and the British Council of Churches. It is on this occasion, one of great joy for his friends in Britain, that CIIR and the BCC take the opportunity to present his rich and stimulating writing to a wide audience in a new publication.

Ian Linden
General Secretary of CIIR

Philip Morgan
General Secretary of the BCC

INTRODUCTION

"Father Ed de la Torre has asked you to write the introduction to the publication of his writings," I was told.

Spontaneously I asked myself, "Why me of all people? He is such a renowned theologian and an international figure."

The last time I saw Ed was at a meeting some three years ago together with priests and religious who were interested in coming up with a theology of the struggle of our Filipino people. I am not particularly close to Ed. In fact, I have not visited him at all like Cardinal Sin and Archbishop Gaviola; not even once, during his detention, neither during the first one or this last one. Perhaps I should.

But I have always asked for news about him and also asked to be remembered to him, in the spirit of solidarity, through his devoted mother, Mommy de la Torre, as friends fondly call her.

I settle for this explanation. Mommy has kept us in touch with each other and perhaps, in her own candid way, close to one another.

It is indeed a privilege to write this introduction to the writings of this man who stands out as a brilliant theologian, a versatile artist, poet, musician and painter.

The name Ed de la Torre was a by-word in the social activism of the sixties. His personal commitment and involvement in the struggle of our Filipino people towards a much-needed and long-overdue social change gave indisputable credibility to his fiery eloquence in rallies, conferences and seminars.

As an outstanding figure he was the object of love and hate. Those who committed themselves to a radical change of our Philippine society admired him, adored him, loved him, hung on to the words that fell from his lips. Those whose vested interests he ran over roughshod hated his guts, calumniated him, despised him, hated him, plotted against him.

When martial law was declared in September 21, 1972, as was expected, the long and mailed hand of the law reached over and grabbed Father Ed to immobilize him. He was detained for more than five years.

His faithful friends and admirers, practically moved heaven and earth to get him released. The effective action of the US Congress got him out of detention and he was set free conditionally. He was to go on "exile" under the custody of his religious superiors.

After a year or so abroad he decided to return and become a part once more of the struggle of the Filipino people, his people. He was then bent on waging the struggle in the field of theology. The Christians who were committed to the struggle of the Filipino people felt the need for theological legitimation of their involvement for radical social change in the face of adverse theological indictment. It was on these grounds that I met Ed again some three years ago.

Like the prophets of the Old and New Testament, Ed has been the rallying point of Christian commitment to the challenging signs of the times, as well as the object of the calumny and ridicule of the powers that be.

As we read his writings, prose, poetry, theological reflections, as we contemplate his paintings, and as we listen to his music, we cannot help, if we approach them with an open mind and heart, but sense a Christian heart beating, full of daring and bold faith in the God of history, who is Yahweh, the faithful One; a brilliant mind that perceives and penetrates in the light of theological faith the puzzling and perplex reality of Philippine society in order to point to the lead of the befriending Spirit; a delicate soul that vibrates with life that struggles to resist death and to overcome it; a spirit that is selfless and dares in the midst of risks that the reign of truth, justice, freedom, love and peace under the God of Jesus-Christ, his God, come about.

Also, following the itinerary of Ed I discover his growth from a reformist to a revolutionary. Let it be understood that revolution simply means radical change. What means are to be used to bring it about, whether parliamentary or armed struggle, is another issue.

Borne out of the hard knocks of life's experience Ed assumes a stand without pretensions, without being dogmatic. His eyes are constantly fixed on the common good of the people and their right to participate in shaping their own history and destiny.

I leave to the readers to discover for themselves in this book the depth of spirit, undaunted courage and richly creative humanity I find in Ed.

† Bishop Julio Xavier Labayen, ocd
Bishop-Prelate of Infanta

Section One

looking back

IN SEARCH OF A FILIPINO THEOLOGY

What do you think brought you to prison?
I was looking for a Filipino theology
You don't land in prison for that! Theology
is not a dangerous enterprise.
It can be. But it's a long story.

Prison Conversation
Camp Olivas 1975

I started writing this at Camp Olivas, some weeks after being arrested on December 13, 1974. A hunger strike to protest torture and indefinite detention got me seven months of solitary confinement, and like other prisoners in isolation I had too many hours that passed too slowly.

Thinking was the easiest way to fill the many days and nights, and impossible to avoid. I worried about the work left undone and companions who would need to regroup in new meeting places. The early afternoon heat would send me to my metal cot, to stare at the ceiling, counting cobwebs, and thanking the spiders for catching those pesky mosquitoes, wondering how many people thought of prisoners that way, before drifting off to sleep. Sunset was always a sad time, despite the bright colors framed by the dark window bars (like Mondrian lines except they were spaced too uniformly). Night brought to mind our many songs and poems especially about freedom surely dawning no matter how long the darkness. Would that the struggle were so simple. But the sun will rise whether we wake or sleep; freedom needs people who keep watch through the night and rouse others, even if they first grumble.

These were the people often in my thoughts, friends and comrades in the struggle, especially those with whom I could identify most closely - middle class Christians who made the passage from reformism to revolution from the mid-60's to the mid-70's. There were enough of us to call a generation, even a first generation, for a second had already begun, those we baptized "martial law babies."

We ought to tell this martial law generation our story, I thought. We had the luxury they didn't have, to openly explore all sorts of theological and political alternatives, without being forced too soon to choose between compromise and clandestiniety. We also had the privilege and burden of having to cut a fresh trail, and while they still had to choose their own way, they had the right to expect some helpful hints from our generation.

There is another group to whom we owe our story - friends, relatives and allies (here and abroad) who supported and sympathized with us through the years even when they did not always understand , no thanks to us. We had the all too common failing of activists who could spend more time patiently explaining ourselves to strangers but presumed that those who know us should accept us without extra effort on our part; perhaps we found it hard to translate into one to one language the issues and options that we could easily discuss in public forums. Even the literature we gave them did not always help, for the movement's writing was dominantly secular, even Marxist, and the occasional Christian pieces did not always

avoid the strident tone that reflected our anger more than the hope within us for which we should account "with gentleness and respect." (1 Peter 3, 16).

OUR story has many beginnings, as many as the individuals of our generation. My part in it dates back to late 1964 after I did my masters in philosophy. I was on regency, teaching Latin, English and Pilipino to high school seminarians in Abra. (Among them were two shy Tingguians who would return as priests to their villages only to be harassed into joining the NPA guerillas). My superiors offered me the choice of applying for theology studies in Rome. I decided not to.

From hindsight, that was a decision that would lead to political involvement. But politics was not yet in my vocabulary then, only theology. I had a vague notion of helping develop a Filipino theology, and felt I had a better chance to do this by staying in the Philippines. Perhaps the preparations for the 400th anniversary of Philippine Christianity (1565-1965) had something to do with that decision; Filipino Christians were in the mood to re-examine what we had to show for those 400 years. I remember agreeing with Fr. Bulatao's insights in his "Socio-Psychological View of the Philippine Christianity," and his critique of split-level Christianity.

Later as activists gathered for *talambuhay* (life story where we exchange accounts of our political development) friends would smile with me at such limited intellectual beginnings. But there were kindred spirits in those early days whose passions were similarly intellectual. They called for a Filipino philosophy and literature, music, theater and art. They made me see my concern for a Filipino theology as part of the more general search for Filipino culture and identity.

Such passion for Filipino culture and identity reflected the spirit of the times, the early 60's. The nationalist movement was starting to gain momentum, drawing in new people and sectors to join those who kept watch through the dark night of the late 50's. "The Second Propaganda Movement" its leaders called it, and like the first propaganda movement of the 1800's it would eventually mature into a revolutionary movement.

OUR circles, however, were not yet politicized then; our nationalism focused on culture and only indirectly related itself to the more central issues carried by the movement - the economic and political domination of the Philippines by foreign powers, particularly the United States. We were not even particularly sensitive to social issues then; not yet.

Even now I still envy those activists whose nationalism quickly articulated itself more comprehensively than ours. Our inchoate nationalism was as much a measure of our intellectual captivity as it was a first stage of awakening. But I find some comfort in what a bishop-friend said. (He was addressing some young, very intense church workers who complained that the church, they meant especially bishops, was asleep, *natutulog*.) "Granted that the Church is asleep, there are different ways of trying to wake her up. We can shout to startle her; I presume you'd want that. Or we can do it more gently, as I tend to do. Let's try both."

I thought of the other angle, the different ways we wake up. Some are almost immediately awake, all nerves alert. Others wake up bit by bit; the eye and the mind clear perhaps, but the body still asleep.

The bishop added, "The Church is more awake than you think. Only, she still needs to get out of bed."

Through the laughter, I thought that had been our saving grace. We got out of bed even though we were not fully awake. We acted on our nationalist consciousness, no matter how limited.

For most of us, the first act was to refuse, an act of negation. (For the movement as a whole, it was to protest). "How negative," critics would remark; "What are you for? What alternatives do you propose?"

Valid questions, all. Someone who says, "I don't want to stay in bed," and struggles to get up may still be asked, "Where are you going?" I don't think we could have answered then, especially not our less politicized group. We were more certain about what we did not want to be anymore. But though we couldn't immediately

present our alternative, we would eventually. For negation, refusal, were precisely the necessary first steps in our search for what we could positively affirm. And those who seek, shall find.

When I learned the language of political economy, I came to understand Philippine theology then as a dependent enterprise, dominated by theologian – merchants, intellectual *compradors* who competed in importing finished products from the West (more precisely, Southern and Northern Europe) for repackaging and retailing locally. In the prevailing division of labor, theological research and production was to be done abroad; our part in the Philippines was "pastoral application."

We could hardly be expected to be content with being theological traders and consumers. We have the right (and duty) to produce our own, a Filipino theology. But how?

The insights came slowly, sometimes with a smile. Some friends once passed by a downtown Manila chapel, its tower topped by concrete letters that proclaimed: *Christ is the answer!* Further down they saw the usual activist slogans, painted loud red; but something else caught their eyes (and fancy), its small letters scribbled with black Pentel pen: *What is the question?*

I thought that was healthy advice to one who was too anxious for answers, for a finished product. If I wanted a really Filipino theology, I should first be sensitive to Filipino questions. These should determine the choice of theological themes, the sequence and stress of treatment.

That meant that I should concern myself not only with a different theology, but with a different method of doing theology.

That shift in emphasis from product to method of production also led me to overcome a bias shared with other intellectuals. We were wont to generalize about *the Filipino* - the Filipino identity, culture, values etc. Usually we were merely projecting our individual visions and passions, or else the limited observations and insights of the circles we moved in. Always we were partial to sources that were in print, especially in books.

Thus my tendency to ask: What are the Filipino questions? What does the Filipino seek? And I would try to find out from printed sources.

Such an approach had two weaknesses. One was that books about the Filipino then suffered from a Western and elitist point of view, with rare exceptions. The other was that the premature abstractions about the Filipino did not adequately represent the rich variety of Filipinos, the many living individuals and groups who together formed the Filipino people.

MUCH later I would understand this latter weakness more precisely as an idealist approach in contrast to a materialist approach. I began to appreciate the efforts of some Marxists to pose the question of materialism vs. idealism not primarily as two sets of contradictory philosophical statements (e.g. spirit over matter and vice-versa) but as two contrasting methods of inquiry. Idealism starts with concepts and abstractions; materialism would proceed empirically, starting with concrete individuals.

And so I learned to ask not about the *Filipino* but first about Filipinos, the many individual Filipinos. Once I did this, I had to look beyond printed sources, to the oral traditions and current conversations of people.

THIS method of using mainly oral sources had social and political consequences for my understanding of theology, not to mention my life.

Because I turned to oral sources, I had to move outside my middle class intellectual (and institutional) setting. So long as I relied on printed sources, I could stay within my limited circles even when reading about the poorer majority of Filipinos. In fact I tended to focus not so much on people but on their abstracted ideas and questions. I dealt with words without flesh and blood.

To rely on oral sources was to seek people where they lived. I would encounter a tremendous variety of Filipinos in various concrete situations, mostly different from mine. I still focused on

their ideas and questions (my conversion to people rather than ideas would be very slow), but I learned not to deal with words except as incarnate - with a voice and face, in specific surroundings.

There is a world of difference between reading the tabulated responses of peasants (N=67) in a sociological report and hearing their heated discussions under an acacia tree in Barrio Dolores, Tarlac. Even the same worker is different when he rides home alone and weary in a jeepney, than when he is explaining issues at a picket line. A mother breastfeeds her baby and has no questions, only prayers at Sunday mass in a Tondo slum; she hurls curses at a demolition crew, her voice rising above her baby's cries.

It is an elementary insight that we cannot fully understand people or their words if we take them out of their concrete conditions of existence. But it was quite a change for me to stop seeking abstract essences and to look for them instead in the multiplicity of social settings and relations.

To experience a variety of individuals and situations was also to perceive the outlines of social categories - rich, poor, not quite rich or poor; elite, masses. Later, class analysis would sharpen and refine them, and I could never again look at the Filipino people as a simple aggregate of individuals. I would relate the individual to the nation always through some intermediate social group, especially the clan (family) and class.

I grew to appreciate the value of basic social organization, if only for the same methodological reasons. Political reasons would come latter. In an organization, the many individuals crystallize their group ideas; they can pose question as *amin* (ours), not only *akin* (mine). I especially cherished the value of a leader who would say *kami* (we), not *ako* (I), and yet was more than mere echo of what every member had said. He distilled their thoughts and feelings and faithfully spoke his people's words, but in his own words.

IT was the questions coming from organized groups and their leaders that pushed the social problems to the center of my theological agenda.

Of course people still asked traditional religious questions: "We are sinners. How can we be saved from sin?" The existing theology then could confidently proclaim: *Christ is the answer.*

But more often the questions, were not that religious: "We are poor and oppressed. Why? How can we be saved from poverty, from oppression? How can we get justice?" Any Filipino theology I would write had to struggle with the social question if I hoped to say *Christ is the answer*, and be faithful both to Christ and the people.

ONE evening, in prison, our desultory talk turned to "the mass line," and mistakes young activists make. A communist party cadre smiled as he reminisced. "We tended to preach rather than listen. I guess because we were so convinced we had the correct line, the answers to the basic problems of the Filipino people." I told about the activist scribbling *What is the question?* We chuckled at the irony.

I added that a Khi Rho activist, I couldn't recall her name, taught me a related insight. She observed that we have two eyes and two ears but only one mouth. Perhaps God was using anatomy to teach would-be theologians and activists a lesson – to observe and listen twice for every impulse to speak. "It's good advice to activists," the CPP cadre agreed; "We should practice it whether we believe in God or not."

A ROAD NOT TAKEN

I spent the summer of '65 with Hanunuo Mangyans in Mansalay, a southern town of Oriental Mindoro. Fr. Anton Postma, the SVD missionary who worked with them, had asked for seminarians to give literacy lessons; he assigned me to an area about five hours' hike away from the poblacion. My first climb, however, took longer. I had to make more than the usual stops to recover my breath and pride, both lost while clutching vainly at vines to break my falls. My Hanunuo guides were properly solicitous, reserving their teasing laughter for later.

The Hanunuos were different from the Mangyans I had known in Naujan, my hometown. I was sacristan to our parish priest when he said mass at Mangyan settlements and those I met were poorly clothed in beaten bark and vines. The Hanunuos wore cotton clothes they themselves wove; their women dyed their skirts indigo blue. I was delighted to find out that they still had their own Malay script (one of only two Filipino ethnic groups to have preserved their pre-Spanish script). They taught me to incise the letters, as they did on bamboo. I hoped I could teach enough of the Latin alphabet in exchange.

I think I wound up learning much more. Fr. Postma shared his studies in *ambahan*, the traditional poems Hanunuos used to express intense feelings of anger or sadness but especially love (the best known *ambahans* were those needed for courtship rites). His own insights and skills were impressive. There was no trace of Dutch accent in his Tagalog; in fact he spoke it with the Batangueño accent of Mindoreños who lived along the coast. He even contributed Tagalog crossword puzzles to *Liwayway* magazine.

He saw his studies about Hanunuo culture as crucial to his missionary work. "I do not want to simply convert and baptize them. I should help them become Mangyan Christians, not just any kind of Christian. Definitely not Western Christians; but not Tagalog Christians either."

That turn in our conversation left me suddenly silent, my mind reaching for words but failing. I felt like my first climb, unable to catch vines to break my fall.

THE idea of a Mangyan Christianity, neither Western nor Tagalog, would continue to intrigue me long after that summer. In much the same way, other fledgling nationalists in search of Filipino culture and identity would be drawn to those we called "cultural minorities." Perhaps overwhelmed by the extent of Western influences on our lowland culture, we longed for a purer, more authentic Filipino culture and hoped to find it in our pre-colonial past, represented by the highland Filipinos who had managed to avoid the wholesale colonization and Christianization of lowland Filipinos.

I remember welcoming the new church hymns based on ethnic minorities' music, especially the *Kyrie* of a Filipino mass which used a Hanunuo *ambahan* chant. Its spare and exotic melody contrasted refreshingly with the more florid Spanish and Italian - influenced church hymns. I couldn't help noticing however (and thinking how curious it was) that the same kind of simpler almost severe melodies were favored also by missionaries who were promoting post-Vatican II liturgical reforms and yet were tapping a different cultural source - Northern European, especially Flemish.

Besides, I had to admit that despite my appreciation for such music I still related more spontaneously and emotionally to those hymns that were most like our lowland folk songs, especially the *kundiman* and the *balitaw*. Was I too much of a lowlander, too Westernized to identify with what I consider the more Filipino music of the cultural minorities?.

A music scholar helped me understand my reactions. He identified five musical strains that together make up what we call Filipino music. The music, of mountain people belong to what he calls the South East Asian strain. It appeals to the Malay within us, a sensibility we share with all Malays in the region. It is the most basic strain and when we call it more Filipino, we mean to emphasize our being Malay, our being Asian.

There are other strains that have resulted from a creative tension between this basic Southeast Asian strain and other musical influences, and these are no less Filipino. There is the Latin-Southeast Asian strain that dominates our lowland folk songs, heavily influenced by Spanish music but not reducible to it. We even have the makings of Filipino pop music, the Afro-American-Southeast Asian strain. (Another observer of our music would write that most Filipino pop singers are half a beat slower than their US counterparts and facetiously attribute it to poorer nutrition). Filipino compositions along classical forms belong to the Teutonic-Southeast Asian strain. Finally, there is the Arabic-Southeast Asian strain in the music of Filipino Muslims in the Southern Philippines.

Other scholars would confirm his insights into the question of cultural minorities and majorities. I had been schooled in the hypothesis that the difference between lowland majorities and highland minorities was based on race. Studies like those of William Henry Scott about the people of the Cordilleras, the cultural minorities, of the North, decisively establish that the colonial subjugation and acculturation of the lowland Filipinos is the historical basis for our division into cultural majorities and minorities.

I did not go back to the Hanunuos after that one summer. It was not a deliberate decision; other activities simply took up my succeeding summers – studies in Philippine church history, workcamps in barrios of the FFF (Federation of Free Farmers), seminars. My search for a Filipino theology did not pursue the path offered by our cultural minorities, again not a conscious choice. Another way beckoned – the organized lowland peasants of the FFF, and that was to be the journey I'd take for many years.

But even that too brief a summer yielded a harvest of insights. A fellow seminarian who watched some Hanunuos transfer a hut *bayanihan* style was moved to compliment them; "You are so ready to help one another; that's very Christian!" He was puzzled, then embarrassed by their sullen reaction. "Don't call us Christians. A Christian is a bad person; it means landgrabber!"

We protested, of course. Landgrabbers were not acting as Christians should; Christians should do good to others. But chastened by the incident, we carefully avoided using Christian as a label of praise from then on. For we had to admit that no matter how we tried to make the

Hanunuo experience kindness from lowland Christians, they had reason to base their judgements on their more frequent and usual encounters with other lowland Christians who shortchanged them. Not to mention history. Some elderly Hanunuos still remembered how their grandparents planted the coconuts that grew near the seashore before they were driven up the mountains by outsiders, those they call *damuong*. We, too, were *damuong* to them; it would take some time for them to call us *kaibigan*, friends.

THE land problem of the Hanunuos was quite serious even then, but my narrow cultural focus prevented me from giving attention to this central issue. Fortunately the next batch of seminarians had previously worked with the FFF and zeroed in immediately on land questions; they were also more technically equipped to help the missionary and the Hanunuos in their efforts to maintain security of tenure and acquire land titles.

Looking back in self-criticism, I can only smile ruefully at my limited cultural concerns that summer - collecting *ambahans*, recording Hanunuo religious myths (like one about a great flood) to compare them with biblical stories, and generally acting like an amateur cultural anthropologist. With that mind-set, I would have eventually poured my energies into writing a book on Hanunuo culture, perhaps even a more ambitious analysis of the encounter between Hanunuo culture and Christian faith. In the meantime , the Hanunuo themselves would have been further dispersed, eventually to disappear as a distinct people, because their land would have been grabbed from them by a combination of sheer force and legal machinations.

Such were the limits of my training that the closest I came to grasping the land problem was to take notes about the Hanunuos concept of ownership. They laid claim only to trees and crops they had planted, not even the land on which these grew. I thought that was one reason why lowlanders could legally cheat Hanunuo of pasture leases. The Hanunuo assumed they were yielding only the grass, not the land itself.

The contrasting sensitivity of the other seminarians to land issues, a product of their work with the FFF, suggested some insights into my method of doing theology. I had earlier thought that all I had to do

was listen, keep myself open to people's questions, then respond from the resources of my Christianity; the result would be a Filipino theology. But listening was turning out to be not a simple, passive process. One can have ears and yet not hear.

Ears need focusing to be attuned to the central questions of the people. I thought of the Thomist principle from philosophy class - "Whatever is received, is received according to the capacity of the receiver". To listen would need more than fieldwork; I would also have to do homework, to acquire and sharpen categories that I need for understanding. In the theoretical language I would later learn, the method of listening is materialist, but not mechanical; it has to be dialectical.

THE need for avoiding a passive, mechanical approach, was brought home by another cultural observation I retain from that summer.

The Hanunuo struck me as a gentle, almost shy, people. Some lowlanders even called them cowardly, for a Hanunuo would rather run away than fight back when hit by a lowlander. But I also saw that they still had spears and arrows tucked behind the corner posts of their huts, though their bamboo shafts were brittle with termite and their metal heads were rusty. Enough Hanunuos still remember which plants to boil for extracting poison.

One can only wonder what series of defeats and futile resistance led to their passive gentleness. Should we judge it as a sign of broken spirits? Or should we understand it as a tactic imposed by unfavorable circumstances?

For a while, there were fields enough to clear for those Hanunuos who withdrew further into the mountains. But the fields were getting smaller and harder to till.

A Filipino anthropologist who came to record Hanunuo culture and also recognized the threat to their existence as a people posed the question to the missionary, a question we all asked ourselves. Surely the Hanunuos had to resist if they hoped to survive; should we not help them recover their culture of resistance?

At least we need not fear we would be imposing alien values; their weapons were witness to their tradition of militancy and struggle.

Besides, the decision to fight would still be theirs. But it seemed safer to merely wait till they fought back and only then support their spontaneous decision; to influence such decision was to share responsibility. (As I write, there is news that the military has tagged the Hanunuo areas as expansion zones of the NPA, the New People's Army. They have ordered the Hanunuos to pledge loyalty in public ceremonies at the poblacion, but continue to treat them with suspicion. Even the missionary has to defend himself against charges of sympathising with the NPA. Unable to stand the constant tension, some Hanunuos can only think of suicide).

The Hanunuos' plight came up in our prison conversation one day in February 1976. We started to brainstorm about a birthday gift for our lawyer, but talk turned to cultural minorities because he was then also involved in the Chico dam issue. My companions were all lowlanders, mostly Ilocanos, who had been NPA organizers among the cultural minorities of the Cordilleras.

I kept thinking of the Hanunuos as they talked about their work with mountain tribes, how deep seated are the differences colonialism has bequeathed, how crucial is the development of local leaders and cadres. We exchanged ideas about building a united front, not only of various classes but also between lowland and highland Filipinos, each tapping a tradition of resistance.

Someone remarked that we were a cultural minority, too, among the lowlanders, at least at the early stages of the struggle before the majority take part. Our lawyer even more so, for the elite circles he comes from do not approve of his politics. That solved our problem about a birthday gift. We gave him a painting of the Igorots at the Chico River area, with a quotation that expressed our bond:

There are times when we must dare to be "cultural minorities" and like them, with them, dare to resist "integration" by those who would plan for us without us.

TO BE A PRIEST, HERE AND NOW
Sermon delivered at first mass, 1968

...Why do we stress our common priesthood? Too often in the past, the priest has been considered a mediator - - standing between a sinful people and an inaccessible God. We looked for God up there, somewhere beyond our reach, and turned to the priest to bridge the gap for us. But God has come down among us; he has become man in Christ. All of us can approach God directly, in Christ.

THIS means that we do not stand between you and God. We stand among you, before God, brothers among brothers and sisters. We are running together with you as members of the human race. We are not bystanders shouting instructions from the sidelines. We are with you. Together we walk as pilgrim church.

For this reason, we need one another. For if we run with you, we can also stumble and fall.

Brave words. Young words. Forgive us our promises. (One of us remarked that we were going to sound like politicians promising to be servants of the people.) But here, as in everything, Christ has given us his example. He did not speak about service, much less define service. He washed the tired feet of his followers.

So we must act, not talk. And yet we must talk! For the primary service the priest can give is to preach the word of God, so that men may answer in faith and form a Christian people, serving men and worshipping God in love.

But if we really mean to serve by our preaching, we must first listen to learn from you. We must learn to listen.

We cannot really be serving you if we only talk and tell you our answers, without asking what your questions are, without listening to what you say, without learning much the answers from you. For after all, we have no monopoly over God's word or his Spirit (even though we bear his image on our vestments). God speaks through everyone of us; the Spirit breathes where he wills.

To really serve you by our preaching, we cannot keep speaking in abstract generalities. We have to apply God's word here and now. We must leave the comfort of universal, general statements, and come down to troublesome particulars. In this way we hope Christianity will reveal its cutting edge as a sign of contradiction that forces us to take sides, to make decisions. Too often, Christianity which should shock people to think and decide, instead makes them yawn and nod to sleep.

Here and now for us is the Philippines, 1968. We have tried to listen to God's word speaking to us in the men and the events of our country. And we believe that all of us have been hard of hearing or have pretended not to hear. For if there is any portion of God's word that Filipinos ask for, it is that word which answers their questions: Why am I poor? Why am I jobless? Why am I treated unjustly? Our class thinks that the Christian social teachings have been kept secret too long. We want to make an explicit effort to preach and practice the social doctrines as the most urgent service asked of us.

This is just part of the greater urgent task that faces us all -- to make Christianity relevant to us Filipinos. And to be really relevant, Christianity must follow the pattern set by Christ. He became man. In the same way, Christianity must become Filipino.

We have to interpret Christianity in terms Filipinos can understand. We must present Christianity in forms our people can recognize as our own. We must preach, we must worship, we must express our faith as Filipinos.

This is a long and arduous task made harder by the fact that Christianity originally came to us by foreign force and not by native acceptance.

But we must try. We especially find it difficult because we have been separated from our people both physically and intellectually. We practically speak a different language. In an effort to stop being strangers to our own people, to reach out and touch you, let me end in a language of our land.

Mahal naming mga magulang. Kami'y inyong mga anak. Kami'y inyo, kaya naibigay ninyo kami sa Diyos. Kami'y naging kaniya; itinuring kaming pag-aari niya. Kaya naman kami'y ibinigay na muli sa inyo ng Diyos, hindi na lamang mga anak, kundi mga pari.

Mga kapwa naming Pilipino. Kami'y binigyan ng Diyos ng kapangyarihan sa pagpapari, hindi upang angkinin at sarilinin namin, kundi ibigay at ipamahagi sa inyo.

Hindi tayo makapagbibigay ng hindi atin. Nguni't ang anumang atin ay atin lamang upang magbigayan - ng buhay, pag-aari, panahon at pagibig - ayon sa kalooban ng atin Ama, na siyang may-ari ng lahat at siyang nagbibigay ng lahat.

(Our beloved parents. We are your children. We're yours and so you were able to offer us to God. We've become His; truly regarded as His own. And so He has given us back to you, not only as His children but also as priests.

Our dear Filipinos. We have been empowered by God as priests, not to serve ourselves, but to serve you.

We cannot share what is not ours. However, whatever we have is ours to share - life, property, time and love - according to the wishes of our Father, who owns everything and shares everything.)

SOME NOTES FOR A THEOLOGY OF SOCIAL REFORM

September 1969

THE Catholic Bishops Conference of the Philippines has come out with an official answer to the SVD Junior Clergy's statement on the social problem. The eighteen-page document provides a starting point for clarifying two frequently misunderstood points: **What is social reform? What is the Church's role in social reform? In the process, I hope to point out some questions for, and answers from, theology.**

Social Reform, Not Social Action

The statement of the bishops' conference mentions the "more than 2000 social action projects...inspired or undertaken by the bishops in the past two years." The Asian Social Institute reports these in detail: housing and resettlement projects, credit unions, cottage industries, miracle rice promotion, model farms, social action seminars, etc. Practically any project that is not purely spiritual and religious is called social action.

But the urgent need of the country is not just social action; it is social reform.

Most of the social action projects are directed at the effects of the social problem. They try to treat the symptoms rather than the disease itself. Social reform aims at the problem itself which is our unjust socio-economic structure.

The basic feature of the social problem is the unjust distribution of wealth. According to reliable economists, 65% of our gross national income goes to only 2.6% of our population (around 130,000 families and a few hundred foreign corporations). The rest of the country (including a negligible middle class) have to share among themselves 22% of the income. The remaining 13% goes to government in the form of indirect taxes.

This maldistribution of wealth and its accompanying maldistribution of power is the social problem of the Philippines. It is a problem of social justice. It calls for social reform.

The urgent need for social reform doesn't remove the need for other forms of social action. Social work, for example, will always be a praiseworthy expression of social concern. But social work is concerned mainly with helping the victims of our unjust society. To engage in it without corresponding action to reform the social structure is to restrict ourselves to mopping the wet floor year in and year out because we do not fix the leaking faucet.

Social reform is not an end in itself. It is but a necessary step to social development. Our socio-economic structure is not only maldeveloped; it is also underdeveloped. But to work for its development without restructuring it would only aggravate the problem. Productivity programs without corresponding justice in sharing and distribution only make the rich richer and the poor poorer in relation to each other.

The Catholic Church in the Philippines has always been in social work. Recently, many churchmen have been involved in productivity and development projects. But the most urgent (and neglected) task facing the Church and the country is social reform. It is so urgent that some writers prefer the term revolution, not so much for its connotation of violence, but to emphasize the need for a rapid radical restructuring of our society.

Why Should the Church Engage in Social Reform?

The very nature of the problem calls for the Church's involvement. Maldistribution of wealth and power is a problem of social justice, a moral problem that demands the Church's concern. Besides, an analysis of the social problem tells us that the maldistribution is not simply the result of natural and historical forces. It is based on unjust concepts of ownership. Hence, the Church cannot refuse direct involvement on the excuse that the problem is mainly technological and economic.

A second reason for involvement comes from the very nature of the Church in the Philippines. The Church is the whole people of God. In the Philippines, then, the Church includes most of those who are suffering from the unjust structures and those who (to say the least) are not suffering from the maldistribution. These include most of us, religious and clerics. If the Church in the Philippines is to be true to her nature — to be a credible sign (sacrament) of Christ's love, it must radically redistribute wealth and power on the basis of social justice and social charity. Otherwise, it can be accused, as the Church in Brazil has been accused, of being in the state of mortal sin.

Closely related to this point is a fact mentioned by a *Graphic* editorial. The majority of Filipinos officially belong to the Catholic Church. The work of social reform which needs the organized action of most Filipinos unavoidably involves at least a significant part of the Church in the Philippines.

Both the nature of the problem (a moral problem of social justice) and the nature of the Church in the Philippines (theological and sociological) demand that the Church engage in social reform. For she is not only part of the actual problem; she is also a significant part of its possible solution.

What Is The Church's Task?

The Church's first task is "to denounce the unjust structures, not as one who judges from without, but one who acknowledges her own share of the responsibility and the blame." These brave words of Archbishop Helder Camara (Recife, Brazil) refer to the whole people of God, the whole Church. But the Church we believe in is also a hierarchical Church, with consequent distinction of roles between laity and clergy. Although the whole Church, all Christians, have the prophetic task of denouncing injustice, the bishops speak with official voices. Hence it is not enough that laymen and priests speak out. They also appeal to the bishops to exercise official moral leadership.

One immediately asks what such denunciation hopes to accomplish. We should first ask what silence in the face of injustice means. Can we blame those who equate it with consent?

In particular, the churchmen's role is to take an active and leading part in awakening both those who profit from the unjust structure and those who suffer from it. In a way, some bishops and priests have started to preach to the affluent to exercise social responsibility. But there has not been equivalent effort to awaken the poor to the needlessness of their poverty and the non-recognition of their rights. When churchmen speak of preaching the social doctrines of the Church, they usually mean telling the rich that they are doing injustice to the poor. But to tell the poor that they are being unjustly treated — this they consider agitation, not preaching. It is against this attitude that Archbishop Camara warns us: "if we omit this — the expression recalls the sin of omission — then tomorrow their eyes will be opened without us and against us. They would consider that they had been abandoned by the Church which was a coward in the face of the powerful, an accomplice of the wealthy who concealed tremendous injustice with generous cult offerings and donations to Christian social activities."

Denunciation and awakening are, of course, not enough. Moral pronouncements alone will not change the situation. There has to be corresponding collective, organized action. But again, here as in preaching, churchmen often think mainly of movements and organizations among rich people. Very few think of awakening the poor to their potential resources and of helping them wield their power in organizations of farmers, workers, "squatters" etc. One wonders if the Church is really the whole people of God, the majority of whom are poor. The impression one gets is that the Church might be *for* the poor, but not *of* the poor.

Serious involvement in the organization of farmers and workers is the answer to the valid objection against the ineffectiveness of mere moral pronouncements. The force that will effectively reform the social structure to give the poor the rights denied them will come from the poor themselves, awakened and organized, exerting not only the moral force of their cause but also the socio-political pressure of their organized numbers.

Toward A Theology of Social Reform

At this point, one might ask where the theology portion of this article comes in. Most of the discussion does not refer to standard

theological *loci* (scripture, tradition, magisterium) and categories.

This is precisely the first feature of any theology of social reform. It has to start with the "signs of the times". Life itself (the social situation) must ask the theological questions, and theology must formulate the answers in dialogue with non-theological sources. This procedure is based on the conviction that God still speaks to us in the problems and events of our times.

A theology of social reform needs to reconcile the concept of social reform with the traditional Christian themes of evangelization, salvation, worship, etc. Otherwise, Christians (and especially churchmen) will refuse to consider social reform as a Christian task, or will engage in social reform for reasons extrinsic to Christianity, e.g. the communist threat.

From Pre-Evangelization to Evangelization

The most primitive rationale for social action is the popular saying "You cannot preach to people with empty stomachs." Some student-demonstrators and many churchmen appeal to this valid theme of catechetics to justify social action. A recent statement of principles issued by an archdiocesan social action council echoed this same thought: social action, though urgent, is not an essential concern of the Church. When the situation is more settled, the Church can turn to more properly spiritual tasks.

We can call such attitude as more properly pre-theological. It considers the gospel (the evangelium) as not yet operative in social action. Christians should help feed the hungry, so that they can listen to the gospel. One wonders if the gospel is restricted to more other-worldly matters.

Perhaps one of the most vocal laymen who insists that social action is evangelization is Atty. Jeremias Montemayor, president of the Federation of Free Farmers. His presentation of this theme is representative of many social actionists all over the world. He points to the passage in *Mater et Magistra* that calls the social doctrine of the Church an integral part of the Christian message. But he is most moving and eloquent when he starts reflecting on two biblical texts:

the Good Samaritan (Luke 10) and the Last Judgment (Matthew 25). Both describe Christian life and salvation as achieved by helping men in their human needs, not just "spiritual hunger, thirst or sickness". Two other points he develops are: love, the center of Christian life, is best tested by helping our neighbor in his physical, material needs. The second is the familiar contrast between "eschatological" and "incarnational" Christianity. The recent controversy about seeking Christ in our neighbor and not only in the Blessed Sacrament is indication that the tension is very real.

Evangelization And Social Development

From concern with *man* (and not just with his soul), we pass on to concern with *men*. Here theology has two choices. It can either reflect on the fact that feeding the hungry is now a social problem, because the problem of hunger is wide-spread and the root causes of hunger are structural, or it can start with directly social theological themes. The late Fr. Camilo Torres started with this gospel passage: "When you come to offer your gift at the altar and you remember that your brother has some grievance against you, leave your gift at the altar and get reconciled with him first. Then come and offer your gift." His reflection on the Mass he was offering and the grievances of the numerous poor against him and against all similarly privileged Christians led him to explore the relationship between the liturgy (our *community* Mass) and social action. I personally find this theme fruitful especially when I have to explain my presence in farmer organizations' meetings. I tell them that we can hardly claim to offer Mass sincerely if our communities are split with injustice. The priestliness of the laity - those who work to build communities by removing injustice and promoting organization - comes into focus. The priest needs the farmer for Mass, not just because he produces the gifts for Mass, but because farmer organizations help form real communities.

These reflections are not based on forced interpretations of isolated biblical texts. The bible passages are simply starting points for exploring organic themes of theology like salvation, worship, community, etc.

If we turn to recent biblical research, we discover that in fact, the main themes of the bible are social. "Salvation, the object of Christian faith in hope, is not a private salvation...The themes of freedom,

peace, justice and reconciliation cannot be reduced to purely internal states or at most I-Thou relationships. They are eminently social and political."

The motto for social development proposed by Archbishop Camara sums up the Christian message: "I am come so that they may have life and have it to the full." Life in its fullest sense is not just spiritual or private. In the happy acronym of the Jesuits, it is SPES - social, political, economic and spiritual.

From Social Development To Social Reform

Up to this point, all we have discussed is the call of the Christian message for social development. The transition to social reform is based on an analysis of existing structures. Since existing social structures prevent social development, then the Christian must work to change these structures; with violence, if necessary. This is the message of such paradoxical slogans as "Peace (development is its new name) Through Revolution".

This transition brings out clearly theology's need to dialogue with non-theological subjects. But we can still ask if there are themes in theology which call directly for social reform, not just as a conclusion from analysis of situations, but as the logical conclusion of theological themes.

Fr. Metz has started working out such themes in his proposal of a political theology. We present a rough outline of his position.

He bases his reflections on the "signs of the times" (modern man's passion for the new that never was) and on the Bible. Although he analyzed not just some passages but the main themes of the Old Testament and the New Testament, we can limit ourselves to two themes. The first is the Kingdom -- the main burden of Christ's preaching. If the kingdom (of peace and freedom, of justice and love) is not yet fully realized here and now, theology and the Church must constantly adopt a critical attitude against any society or system that pretends to be final or set against change. Together with this theme of the kingdom as the ideal on which we base our criticism of the "world", Metz develops the biblical theology of asceticism, exemplified by St. Paul's warning, "Do not be conformed to this world." Since

Christians obviously cannot fly away like astronauts from the world, they cannot but conclude that not being conformed means to seek to change the world -- to make peace, freedom, justice and love more and more present in society.

Metz describes the Church's function as institutional criticism -- a permanent critic of society who can never passively accept present structures. Christians must continually work for change, constantly reminding themselves of the very eschatological themes that have misled other Christians into unconcern about the problems of this world.

This inadequate summary is basis enough for an immediate conclusion about social reform. It includes and demands Church reform. For the Church, too, must judge herself against the ideals of the Kingdom to which she must give way. Besides, the Church is not completely "other" from the world, especially in the Philippines with her numerous members.

This last point is perhaps one of the most painful and yet necessary aspects of social reform. Christ's preaching of the kingdom included a call for repentance, conversion. The central theme of our faith is the paschal mystery; and for all the present stress on the resurrection, it still starts with suffering and crucifixion. If there is anything we must first do, as a first step in social reform, it is to confess our guilt and admit our fault. This is what is disturbing about the answer of the hierarchy. The whole tenor is one of self-justification. But all of us are at fault -- the whole Church, bishops, priests, religious, the affluent laymen and even the poor (indirectly, by being passive cooperators in the oppression inflicted by others). The sooner we admit our sinfulness, the sooner we can hope for a Christian renewal of our country.

THE ROLE OF THE PRIEST IN SOCIAL REFORM

September 1970

THE original topic assigned to me was "The Priest and the Social Apostolate." I have narrowed down the topic to social reform because the term social apostolate is too general for discussion. Besides I do not have any special experience in the other fields of social apostolate.

But there is a deeper reason for focusing on social reform. Fr. Villote's survey (PPF Dec. 1969) asked 205 Filipino secular priests the following question: "What are you doing, Father, to solve the social problem of our country?" He noted that there were about as many projects mentioned as there were priests interviewed. This remark and the different lists of projects that get reported every so often in the press seem to indicate confusion about the nature of "the social problem" of our country.

When priests and bishops talk of "the social problem," very often they refer to *social problems,* meaning any widespread, not purely spiritual, problem (juvenile delinquency, poverty, ill-health, crime and unemployment). They wonder why in spite of numerous social action projects people accuse them of not solving the social problem. They think it is a matter of lack of publicity. Perhaps it is more accurate to say that it is lack of direction.

Maybe this incident will help spell out the difference between social problems and *the* social problem. This happened at a medical dispensary in Tagaytay City. A farmer once came with an eye disease; the brother-in-charge treated him and sent him away cured. After a few weeks, the same farmer returned, this time with an ear disease. He got cured after a couple of treatments. But without fail, the same man and some other patients would come back with some other ailments.

The brother-in-charge decided to investigate these patients' background to find out why they had so many sicknesses. He finally told us that the main problem of these patients was their weak resistance to any disease; their undernourished bodies simply could not fight the different bacteria that caused the sicknesses.

To talk of the *social problem* is to go beyond individual problems to the over-all weakness of the country's structure.

What are the reasons for this weakness? The first reason usually given is that the Philippines is underdeveloped (or in the propaganda of the West – "developing"). The other and more specifically social problem is that the Philippines is not only underdeveloped but also maldeveloped.

If we picture the country as a Filipina maiden, then we would see a rather pretty head that is too big and out of proportion to the thin body. To shift from picture to statistics, we read that only 2.5% of our

people get 65% of the total income of our country. This 2.5% is made up of around 130,000 families (further allied into extended family blocs), and a few hundred foreign corporations. More important than their overwhelming share of the country's income is their ownership and control of the sources of income (land, factories, means of production).

This economic maldistribution has resulted in maldistribution of power — social, political, and even military (in warlord territories). This concentration of power on the side of a few leads to further opportunities of accumulating wealth: buying of lands, controlling industry, often using public funds for private investments.

To complete the cycle, we have to add the maldistribution of cultural and educational and even religious opportunities.

Thus we see two vicious cycles in our country. One, a cycle of wealth-education-power and the other a cycle of poverty-ignorance-powerlessness. This separation has reached the physical-geographical stage: the elite withdraw into exclusive barrios with their own police, shopping centers,and recreational facilities.

This mal-formed structure (socio-economic, political, cultural) constitutes the social problem of the Philippines. It is aggravated by the fact that our country is entangled in the web of international economic imperialism. This refers to the alien control of our strategic industries, the exploitative nature of foreign investments (mainly domestic borrowing with shipping out of profits), and consequent political pressure on government policies (with the help of willing Filipino partners). It also includes the unbalanced international trade relations decried by *Populorum Progressio:* the Philippines is one of the countries which are mainly suppliers of raw materials and primary products that are subject to fluctuating prices in the "free market" dominated by developed countries whose manufactured exports continually increase in price.

In the face of the social problem, let us examine what people mean when they talk of solving the social problem.

The most commonly used term is SOCIAL ACTION. Practically any organization that wants to show current concern goes into social action. *Action NOW* once announced: "The Metrocom goes into social action." Social Action covers a lot of projects, from planting

mushrooms to community development. A common feature seems to be this: a welcome shift from concern with man's purely spiritual needs (his soul) to caring for his human needs.

However, a survey of announced social action projects reveals that (a) there is less action than what is announced in so many publications and press releases and (b) the action is not always social in the sense of being widespread and organized.

Most social action projects are in the nature of SOCIAL WORK. This refers to outright doles and alms (Christmas fund drives, help to fire victims), to medical care and recently to some self-help projects.

Perhaps the field which is relatively new for bishops and priests is the field of productivity and technology. This partakes of the nature of social work but has its proper characteristics. Some examples would be irrigation projects, model farms, fertilizers, piggeries and cottage industries.

Some priests and seminarians have actually gone into farming to demonstrate to other farmers the latest methods in agriculture. This has led people to comment: *"Baligtad na ang mundo! Ang pare ang nagsasaka; Ang cursillista ang nagsesermon."* (The world is upside down! The priest goes into farming; the *cursillista* preaches.)

Apart from the question of roles, we have to point out that the Philippines' social problem does not refer primarily to its under-development (to be solved by production and technology) but to its maldevelopment (justice, redistribution of wealth and power). In fact an increase in GNP (over-all weight) might even indicate a worsening social problem (the head growing too big in relation to the thin body).

This brings us to the need of SOCIAL REFORM. What does social reform really mean? It is at once specific and general. Specific, because it directs itself at structural changes (economic, political, educational, cultural, even religious). Such change is more often called revolution. Unfortunately, the term revolution has been limited to connotations of military violence; on the other hand, reform gives the impression of a few, slow surface changes. Here we take reform in the sense of *Populorum Progressio:*

"One thing is certain, the present situation must be faced courageously, and the injustice it comprises must be fought and overcome.

Bold transformations and profound changes are the price of development. Reforms must be urgently undertaken, without delay. Everyone must generously play a part."

The passage illustrates the two aspects of social reform. It is at once specific (direct structural changes), and yet general (everyone must and can do his part). In other words, although economic and political relations (the direct target of social reform) constitute the core of the social problem, they have so interacted that they have spawned secondary problems now in turn aggravating the main problem. Hence acting for the betterment of society, e.g., education, moral regeneration, in some way contributes to social reform. On the other hand there are certain activities that are more directly and immediately part of social reform.

At the top of the list is the reformation of the power structure. This is primarily political but includes economic and social aspects. The reformation of the power structure is to my mind more basic than economic development of the poor. The question is not simply that justice should be given to the poor but who is going to do it.

Will it be done for the weak by socially concerned people in power? Here Christian social thought is rather explicit. Development cannot be imposed from outside. Reform cannot be simply given from top. If that happens, it is not development but paternalism (almost as bad as exploitation).

The poor people themselves must be awakened to their rights, organized to gather their voice and strength in order to denounce the unjust structures and effectively reform society.

I am personally committed at present to the belief that reforms can be achieved by socio-political organizations of farmers (tenants, settlers), workers (agricultural and industrial), "squatters", and youth. Other serious-minded people in the Philippines disagree and claim that those in power are too inflexible and will resist change. They have therefore opted for direct destruction of the power structure by violence.

Priests in Social Reform

Before we talk of the role of the priest in social reform, perhaps we should first resolve the question: Why should a priest be in social

reform at all? Is it his proper field? Is this not the task of the government or the citizens?

First of all, before a priest is a priest and even as a priest he is a Christian and a man. The social problem is the concern of every Christian and every man in this country, and we cannot give the answer of a priest-professor who was asked why he didn't care about the social problem: "Oh, it's not my line."

But we can still ask: should we be in social reform precisely as priests? We are not trained to be economic or political leaders. Should social reform not be the job of a few specialists?

To ask that question is to ask the ticklish question of what the priest essentially is. What his essential priestly functions are as distinguished from the priestly people of God.

Let us bypass that unfinished discussion by limiting ourselves to the priest's role as leader of the worshipping community. This function is at least relatively secure. The priest is leader of the cult, presiding officer at the liturgical assembly especially at Mass.

The late Father Camilo Torres once wrote some reflections on the relationship between the Mass and Social Reform. His remarks were occasioned by a passage in the gospel according to St. Matthew.

If you are bringing your offering to the altar and there remember that your brother has something against you, leave your offering there before the altar, go and be reconciled with your brother first, and then come back and present your offering. Mt. 5, 23-24

He wrote: "Everyday at my Mass I offer my gifts at the altar; so do most good Christians on Sundays. But most of our brothers (who are poor, who do not go to Church) have a lot of things against us, for we all belong to privileged classes. Should we not get reconciled with them first?"

We know that after being frustrated in his attempts at social reform, he dramatically announced to the press that he would stop offering his Mass in an unjust society. He then decided to join the revolutionaries.

A lot of young men and women with whom I have worked and who want to be Christians engaged in social reform agree that this reflection might be the deeper reason for their rejection of Mass and

liturgy as meaningless. "It is not simply a question of songs or prayers or imported forms and rites. The Mass is supposed to be a community Mass. What if there is no real community? What if the society is split with justice?"

When farmers ask me to explain my presence (and the Mass) at their meetings, I usually refer to this reflection. We used to tell them that the priest needs the farmer for Mass because the gifts we offer are the produce of farmers (at least in other countries). But there is a deeper need of the priest for farmers, especially farmer organizations. First, because these organizations are real communities bound together by common aspiration for justice, and secondly, because by generating power these organization can restore justice and the balance of power that will heal our split communities. Here we get a glimpse of what the priestliness of the laity means. They help build and form the Christian community.

There is a second specific reason for priests' involvement in social reform. The social problem is not just an economic and political problem. The social problem is, at its core, a moral problem. It is a problem of social justice. Not only is it as such unjust. One of its deepest roots is an unjust concept of ownership, especially of land.

The Role of the Priest in Social Reform

From the preceding discussion, one might get the impression that the priest should now start organizing farmers, workers and youth. The more reasonable conclusion we should make is this: We should tackle the problem of social justice and get involved in organizations that are working for social reform.

More specifically, the priest's role is not to plant or to plant but to preach. That is his primary role whether before or after Vatican II.

Once we talk of preaching we think of the pulpit and church goers and so unavoidably limit ourselves to reaching the upper and middle class. In fact, this is what we usually think of when we are asked to preach the social teachings of the Church: to tell the rich to exercise social responsibility (*Maawa naman kayo.* Give justice to the poor). But we don't give equal time (and their numbers would demand more of our time) to preaching the social gospel to the poor, to awaken them to their rights and to the need to demand their

rights. For most of us, for most Christians, this sounds suspiciously like agitation.

But it is not enough that justice is given: it must also be *asked* for.

Very recently I realized with a shock that in the past months I have been talking mainly to students, professionals, sisters, priests and Rotarians rather than preaching to farmers, workers and settlers.

What to preach? The social gospel. Here we are faced with a problem. Hardly anyone of us had a seminary course on Christian social teachings (a lack that seminaries are only starting to remedy). But instead of wringing our hands and blaming our inadequate training we all simply have to learn as we go along.

More than reading books and attending seminars and listening to lectures on social matters we should give double time to listening and learning from the poor themselves not just what the social problem is but also the answers to the problem. (The spirit breathes where He wills). Essential therefore to effective preaching is our living presence among the poor. I think it was Father Villote who once said that if we Catholics really believe in a visible Church, then the Church leaders should be visible in the barrios and in the slums.

The second function is the formation and motivation of leaders.

The common objection against mass organizations is that their leaders are irresponsible; that they tend to abuse their power. Perhaps they are irresponsible, but that does not take away the fact that organization is a natural right of man. It is also a constitutional, legal, and moral right as attested to by our laws and the encyclicals. Moreover in an unbalanced society, organization of the poor becomes a duty.

Very often, what people consider as abuses of organizations is only the "unnatural" stance of a farmer or a worker speaking like a man, not begging for, but demanding his right.

But if there is real irresponsibility (and there is), whose fault is it that leaders are not properly formed? The moral leaders, definitely, and the Catholic schools as group. Our schools do produce leaders but only for a very limited sector of society. A school for farmer leaders? Labor leaders? We do not even encourage our youth leaders to plunge into social reforms as a logical outcome of their Christian faith.

In connection with mass organizations, the priest has a peculiar function in present Philippine society: to counteract the inevitable accusation that such organizations are communist or leftist. It is unfortunate (although flattering to communists) that any movement that is militant is immediately suspected and accused of being Red, especially if it is a movement of the poor. Strangely enough, when we think of Christian movements our immediate reaction is to picture it as a movement of the elite.

The third specific function of the priest (and this is the most painful task) is moral pronouncement and exertion of moral pressure. This is the role of prophecy that many laymen have asked Churchmen to play. To courageously denounce injustice, point out who is wrong and take sides with the oppressed – these are what manifestoes and speeches of laymen, especially the youth, have challenged Christian bishops to do.

This task of moral pronouncement need not always be public and dramatic, although perhaps our society and our Church need such shocks. Some quiet firm types can tell landlord, bishop, religious or businessman that he is not just illegally but even more unjustly ejecting his tenant or busting unions and underpaying workers.

The immediate objection to such a role is that it is ineffective. Of course, if all we do is talk we can shout ourselves hoarse and the situation will still remain the same. But the moral pronouncement is not supposed to be directed at the rich people alone. It is not only denunciation of injustice or telling them to give justice. It is also reassuring the poor of the justice of their cause and the need to organize. This calls especially for a clear explanation of the Christian view on conflict and struggle.

The force that will effectively bring about change will be generated by the lay people especially the poor themselves. But even if there were no such effective organization yet, priests and bishops are still expected to speak out against injustice if only to sever the silent alliance between the Church and the status quo. As a labor leader from Negros put it: "Tell the hacenderos that to prevent unions of hacienda workers is a mortal sin. Perhaps they will not listen, but that is their privilege. All we ask is that the Church's stand should be very clear."

Silence in the face of injustice still looks suspiciously like consent.

Some Problems and Proposals

The first area of difficulty is the relationship between the priests and laymen in social reform. Are the priests to exercise leadership in Christian social reform movements? The answer of the lay leader is very clear. The priest should not exercise organic leadership. Organizations of tenants, settlers, workers and youth are the work of laymen.

The priest's role is important but limited. Apart from personal charisma, the priesthood and our seminary training do not give us any special competence in the field of social reform. I am rather fortunate to be working with laymen who have accepted me and have helped to determine my role. But I have also talked with labor and youth leaders who have practically slammed the door on priests because some of them wanted to be the "fathers" of their organizations.

Perhaps the attached guidelines for priests' role in the Federation of Free Farmers can serve as an example of how the problems of priest-lay relationship in social reform could be solved. We must realize, however, that the field is relatively new and therefore guidelines are at best provisional.

The second and more pressing problem is the relationship of the priests to their bishop.

The call to exercise moral leadership was first directed to bishops since they are supposed to be the moral leaders of the community and our priesthood is to a great extent only a participation in theirs. But in spite of their attempts to disclaim it, bishops still act in such a way as to merit Martin Luther King's remark about the Christian Church in general that instead of being the headlight that points out the way, it has acted like the tail light (speaking out only to stop those who are getting too "imprudent").

I don't want to explore this topic now. I only want to point out that some priests who would want to be in social reform and started to work in this field were not only not encouraged by their bishops but even suffered disciplinary action. On the other hand there are also some bishops who have courageously tried to fulfill their role together with their priests.

This leads me to the main proposal I like to make. It concerns the PPI as a national organization of priests.

If there is any aspect of social reform that has been stressed in this paper, it is the need for organization. Therefore an individual priest trying to exercise his role alone especially by giving moral pronouncement cannot hope to be as effective as when he is connected to an organization. For some it might be the lay organization of which he is chaplain or adviser. For others it might be (should be) the religious order or a diocese to which he belongs. But in default of those two could the PPI not serve to provide the encouragement and institutional force that an organization gives?

Pope John said that a solitary voice speaks to the winds. Perhaps that is what deters priests from speaking out. Perhaps that is the reason why laymen have the impression that the moral leaders, specifically the priests, are silent about the social problem. But if a national organization of priests would take it upon itself to speak out on the social problem then we can hope that more priests and laymen would work together for social reform.

The PPI has been working admirably for the collective security of priests. It is equally in a position to exercise collective prophecy.

APPENDIX

The Role of the Chaplain in the Federation of Free Farmers

The chaplain shall have no organic power in the secular activities of the FFF. Thus, the chaplain will have no power to vote in the meetings of the National Policy Board or other branches of the FFF, nor will he be committed by any resolution or action taken thereby. In other words, the chaplain will have no organic say as to whether or not the FFF, for instance, should declare a strike, or whether to file a particular case in court or not, or whether to support this or that political candidate, or whether to buy a tractor or not.

But the chaplain has the right and duty to speak and to be heard on all *moral aspects of any such questions.* For instance, if he clearly believes that filing a particular case is immoral, he must say so to the proper FFF officials. And the FFF should not stop him from saying so. On the other hand, the FFF will still be free to decide whether to file the case or not, taking in mind, however, the advice of the chaplain. As will be made clear, the action taken by the FFF will not

commit the chaplain; but it could happen that the matter may be an extremely serious one and the chaplain cannot in conscience continue to be such while the FFF proceeds along a certain line of action. In such a case, the chaplain can resign any time and the FFF cannot compel him to remain a chaplain.

The specific functions of the chaplain are: 1) moral guidance and spiritual advice; 2) moral formation and motivation or inspiration; 3) exertion of moral influence; and 4) religious services.

Yet, it must be emphatically stated that an ordinary priest is a highly intelligent person capable of giving good advice even in secular or semi-secular matters. Thus FFF officials may even seek the advice of the chaplain with respect to the purchase of a particular kind of tractor. If he has special knowledge of the matter, nothing will prevent the chaplain from giving his advice if he wants to.

Moreover, under special circumstances the FFF may request the chaplain to perform an organic function in the FFF like organizing an FFF chapter or cooperative unit, or acting as treasurer of a certain project, etc. Even without these special arrangements, the chaplain can always *encourage* the various activities of the FFF.

In order that the chaplain can perform his duties properly, he has the following rights in the FFF:

1. To attend all meetings of the FFF from the lowest to the highest level.
2. To have access to all papers of the FFF except those that are confidential in nature.
3. To be received as an official of the FFF in any function, occasion, party, program, as well as in any member or leader.
4. To be received as a friend by all members and leaders of the FFF and their families.
5. To be listened to by the FFF leaders and members whenever he gives moral advice, except when it is directed to non-Catholics and the advice does not concern FFF matters.
6. To organize retreats, devotions, live-ins, and other projects within the FFF in fulfillment of his functions as described above.
7. To require organizational support and facilities within the capacity of the FFF for all activities falling under his role as described above.

DISCOVERING THE FILIPINO AS PEASANT

IN April 1980, I was released from prison with the understanding that I should go to Rome for studies. I couldn't help smiling at the irony. The long journey that led me to prison had started with a decision not to study theology in Rome.

Despite that decision to stay and pursue my search for a Filipino theology in the Philippines, I had to accept the possibility of leaving the country for a foreign mission assignment, as demanded by the SVD's missionary character. I remember drafting a farewell speech for such an event, even quoting a half-remembered poem of Rizal about a plant suddenly uprooted: *Yo soy planta/apenas crecida/ arrancada del Oriente* (I am a plant/hardly grown/uprooted from the Orient.) In 1980 it would be Bonifacio's poem that spoke to me: *Sa aba ng abang mawalay sa bayan/Gunita ma'y laging sakbibi ng lumbay/Walang alaala't inaasam-asam/Kundi ang makita'y lupang tinubuan.*

Plant and soil -- elemental images in my search. Rizal had a fable about the monkey who thought he was clever to seize the leaves and fruits of a banana tree, leaving the trunk and roots to the turtle. Filipino intellectuals are like that, an FFF leader would tell me, fruits and flowers that crown a tree. But what gives the tree its strength are the roots. Without healthy roots, flowers and fruits will shrivel and die. So long as roots remain healthy, you can cut the branches and there will be new growth. The nation's roots are the peasants, hidden and muddy, but the source of the new sprouts that we seek.

Now I think of the Filipino as a complex sum of many classes, but then I could accept the simple equation of the Filipino as peasant. One reason is numbers; the majority of Filipinos are peasants.

Another reason is the peasant's links to the land. I share the feeling (one writer calls it agricultural fundamentalism) that those who work with the land are somehow more human, more whole.

I met the Filipino as peasant in the Federation of Free Farmers. For at least four years (1967 to 1970), I held a simple chain of propositions: The majority of Filipinos are peasants. Their main problem is the land problem. The main solution lies in organizing the peasants to struggle for justice. The biggest organization of peasants is the FFF. Work with the FFF and you address the central questions of the Filipino.

For a whole generation of middle class Christian activists, church people and lay, the FFF offered just the right political and ideological stance we could identify with. Within the FFF, we met peasants not as atomized conservatives (not Marx's sack of potatoes), but as organized militants who were sufficiently class-conscious to identify an enemy system by name -- feudalism or landlordism. Its leaders were reassuringly reformist (many of them were middle class like us), although we would also satisfy our need to be called radicals by telling each other we were dealing with the root problems of the grassroots. The FFF was also explicitly inspired and guided by social principles drawn from papal encyclicals, even though pro-landlord church people accused it of being communist. (One of the ironies of Christian reformism is that it is always suspected as communist even if it is partly motivated by anti-communism, as the FFF was). As the FFF reached out for support from the student youth, it even used Mao Zedong's writings as a kind of left-handed confirmation of its work, citing Mao's emphasis on peasants as the main force in the new democratic revolution, while downplaying his recognition of the proletariat as the leading force.

Even after 18 years I can still feel the impact of that encounter. For alienated urban intellectuals, the organized peasants represented the roots of our Filipino identity. In the FFF, I met the peasant not just as suffering, but as struggling -- the twin traditions that combine to ground me emotionally. Amid that swirl and flow of feelings, there was also intellectual excitement, as both peasant and non-peasant leaders posed fresh and forceful questions. I would thank them for pulling me out of the sheltered intellectual confines of the seminary *kung saan pumutla na pati utak* (where even the brain becomes pale)

and for exposing my mind to the sun, to make it again *kayumanggi* (brown-skinned).

In contrast, the prevailing theology, then, appeared to me like a potted plant, rooted in special soil, remote from the rich deepest layers of peasant consciousness. As I travelled from one FFF chapter to another, hearing a question asked in Davao that echoed a question posed in Bulacan, picking up a fragment of an answer in Laguna that fit another fragment from Negros, I felt the fear and trembling that told me I was finally in dialogue with an authentic part of the Filipino soul.

As far I can recall, the conversation started in Laguna, just as the sun was setting. An FFF leader joined me at a *sari-sari* store. He had a couple of drinks (*pampaliwanag ng isip* - for clearing one's mind - we used to call it) and felt comfortable enough to tease me as he was wont to. "If you really want to understand us", he winked at me, "you should raise your own family." I fended that off with smile. Did he have any other advice for a priest who wanted to preach to peasant leaders like him, so they would listen and not leave the chapel for a smoke during the sermon?

"You priests say the same things: Go to mass. Don't gamble. Don't get drunk. Don't sleep with any woman except your wife. You preach only about my weekends and my night life! But day in and day out, morning till evening, I am a farmer - plowing the field, harrowing, planting, weeding, spreading fertilizer or spraying pesticide. Why is there no sermon about that?"

Back in Tagaytay, at the seminary, I would translate his tirade to my professor. "He's saying that we address only the fringes of his life, not its center. He's saying we should speak to him as a farmer. That's central to his identity as a human being, as a Filipino."

Another FFF leader asked: "When I harvest 40 cavans of palay per hectare, am I a better Christian than one who harvests only 29 (the national average? " I told myself, "He's asking for theology of development! "

When the FFF started its retreat for farmers at the Pope John XXIII Training Center, I was usually asked to give a talk on the "theology of

work". The first time I had to give it, I rushed to the library only to find just a single slim book on the topic, plus a section in another commentary on the social encyclicals.

I would usually start with Genesis, the very first verse of the bible giving the very first image of God. God is at work, not in contemplation, making heaven and earth. He makes man to his image, as co-creator. God is the source of all life, but human life comes into the world only through people's cooperation. No baby is born except through the love of man and woman. So also the fruits of the earth. They need people who till and plant and harvest.

Someone usually teases me. "Why don't you help bring new human life into our world? You're not obeying God's command to increase and multiply!" That starts a round of banter. Then someone always asks: "If work is according to God's will, how come it is so hard?" That provokes a more serious discussion. Inevitably, talk turns to the passage about Adam being condemned to live by the sweat of his brow. "You mean to tell us, work is punishment for sin? You mean those of us who sweat under the sun are more sinful than the landlords?"

At this point, it is I who would be sweating. There were big words in my head, especially "alienation". When I didn't know any better, I caused headaches (honestly reported during evaluation) with my tortuous intervention. Later, I learned to let them sort things out themselves.

In the process, a lot of other issues got pulled into the heated exchange, including baptism. That was because of the reference to sin. They complained about having to wait till fiesta time before the priest visited their barrio. But they saw pictures in the newspaper of priests, even bishops, blessing factories and buildings, with plenty of holy water sprinkled around. Perhaps the church considered buildings as more important than babies? Or, maybe those buildings (and their owners) had more sins that needed to be washed away?

We'd wind up agreeing on two points. Work, and not just prayers, can be saving and holy. But not within a system that gives others the right to take away the fruits of our work. We need to change such a system to one that gives proper recognition to the value of work. To

struggle for such change is holiness.

Perhaps the strain of the intense debate made them vulnerable. I never knew the precise reason. But always, at this point, there would be tears. Not flowing, just enough to quickly wipe with a finger or blink away. I always felt slightly embarassed, worried I might be manipulating them like a *rollista* during Cursillo. I don't think it was anything particularly eloquent I said, although the image of the peasant as the roots of the nation visibly moved them.

During the evaluation, FFF leaders had a partial answer. It's inner realization of their dignity as peasants, and their importance for the whole nation, and the value of their struggle. "We arrived at this ourselves", they said. "We didn't need you to tell us that. But hearing it from you, a priest, is a confirmation from a source we want to hear it from, but rarely do."

That answer contained another question that would confront us later. The spirit of post-Vatican II made us shed our cassocks for ordinary clothes; we used traditional garb only for mass and other official functions. But to show solidarity with FFF members, we wore our cassocks at court hearings and demonstrations. That led to accusations of using religious symbols for partisan purposes, doing for the "left" what others previously did for the "right".

FFF leaders reassured us that they welcomed that kind of partisanship, and it was easy to brush aside questions that came from hostile conservative quarters. Among ourselves, however, we also wondered about what we called "neo-feudal" or "neo-clerical" relationships with the peasants. It was easy to justify the distribution of quotations from papal encyclicals and church fathers to landlord *cursillistas* and share the satisfaction of Mang Peping at their discomfiture and inability to call him a communist, since he quoted Ambrose and Chrysostom. At one seminar in Davao, the FFF recruits even asked me to give them the Latin titles of the encyclicals. I started with *Rerum Novarum,* and one of them exclaimed that it sounded like thunder, *parang kulog*! He couldn't wait to hurl it at his landlord.

Were we not creating a new dependence, just when the peasants were freeing themselves from their old captivity? We recognized the temptation, but felt that the use of church authority served the

peasants' transition from resignation to struggle. We knew well enough that it was their perception of their condition that pushed them to seek change, but we also knew that it was not only the physical risks of the struggle that made them hesitate. There were inner doubts, reflecting the chains of the mind. I felt sad and angry that a peasant should ask: "Did the Pope really say that? That we must organize and fight? It's not a sin?" Boy Ipong, an ex-seminarian who found his new vocation with the FFF, talked of the need for the peasant to kill the landlord inside him, echoing Freire. He thought that was one way to interpret the Bible passage about the old man dying so that the new man may live.

We didn't kill the landlord in the peasant. Only the peasant could do that, and be really free. But I think we gave him some of the weapons he needed.

The peasants gave us weapons, in turn, for the killing that we had to do within us. When church authorities branded us communist, we simply laughed that off, because deep inside we knew we were not. But when they accused us as unchristian because we took sides, because we excluded the landlords from our caring, we were vulnerable. We still carried within us the self-image of the church as mother of all, peasant and landlord alike, and the church as mediator, pontifex, bridge-builder.

The peasants' rebuttal was sharp as a sickle: "So, the church is our mother? Doesn't a good mother take the side of her younger, weaker son, defending him against the bullying of the elder son? As for building bridges, did you ever try to build a bridge by starting at the middle?" Through the laughter, I told myself these are really *ad hominem* arguments. They still concede the church's self-image as above classes. But they are just right for the kind of people who continue to invoke such an image.

ANOTHER conversation started in Pampanga and continued in Negros. When I was still anxious to present a finished theological product, I called this conversation a "theology of land".

It started with an FFF leader's remark about what he called the peasants' "moral instinct" on social issues. They have a gut

feeling about what's right and wrong, what should be, rather than simply what is. But they need to articulate this, and often turned to the church for help, since they expected moral issues to be couched in religious terms. Like flesh seeking to become word.

One of the peasants' deepest feelings is about land. He feels that those who till the land should be recognized as owners. The slogan "land to the tiller" says it, but the land reform law did not match their expectations.

The FFF leader asked: "Suppose a peasant goes to his parish priest. He asks for a bible text that justifies his wanting to own the land he tills. Or better, a text that says he is in fact the owner because he tills it. Do you think the priest can give him one? I am afraid that the priest will end up warning him with the commandment - thou shall not covet your neighbor's goods."

With such pro-landlord bias in the church, it was easy for an HMB organizer to preach his gospel to the peasant in the late 1940s. He'd ask why the land that the peasant tills is considered the landlord's property. Because it is the law; the landlord has the title. Why? Because he inherited it from his father, just as his father inherited it. Why does the landlord inherit land, while the peasant inherits only debts? "Trace that title and you'll find that it was first given to the bastard son of friar! Why? Because the first land titles were royal grants from the King of Spain. The Americans legalized them with Torrens title."

The HMB organizer would then deliver his clincher: "Who gave the King of Spain the right to distribute land in the Philippines? The right of conquest. Well then, if we want to take back the title, we need guns."

The FFF leader agreed that the HMB's message is definitely better than "Thou shall not covet." Still, it doesn't seem right. A gun might be the ultimate title, but someone can come with a bigger gun. There is truth to the insight that law reflects the prevailing power arrangements, but power is not all. There must be principle.

What principles there were, we studied with students before their summer workcamps in FFF barrios. God is the only absolute owner of all the earth, and His will is that the earth should belong to all God's children. Human ownership can only be stewardship, and the right to use has primacy over the right to own. Standard material from the encyclicals.

From moral theology came further principles. What determines ownership? The nature of what is to be owned, and its relative scarcity or abundance. Labor and need. How much land does a person need? In death, six feet. In life? Neither in death nor in life was there land for everyone's need. The rich had memorial parks; the poor were often piled on top of each other. Given the ratio of land to people in the Philippines, how many hectares is a mortal sin?

Even Marlon Brando joined the conversation, in his movie *Viva Zapata.* A Mexican peasant was shot as he tried to cut barbed wire that fenced him from his corn field. As his wife and child cried over his body, someone asks why he risked his life for his land. Did he not think of his wife and child? "For a farmer, land is like a woman. It is difficult to live with her for such a long, long time, only to be told in the end that she's not your own."

I thought the words could have come just as easily from a Central Luzon peasant. But it was a peasant from Negros whose story became a poignant commentary to that line from the movie.

Louie Jalandoni, then Negros FFF chaplain, told of a farmer who needed legal assistance. He was brought to court by a *hacendero* who had decided to expand his sugar plantation to marginal land, to take advantage of the rising price of sugar in the world market. Years before, the farmer had cleared a piece of forest land, not knowing it was already titled in favor of the hacendero. The farmer cried in helpless rage: "If I had known then that you owned that land, I would not have spent so many years cultivating it!" The hacendero's lawyer was moved to some sympathy. But we have to follow the law, he said. *Dura lex, sed lex.*

The story agitated us all. What if there was a hacendero who saw a peasant girl, liked her enough to marry her, but left her virgin, like that forest that the farmer found? While the hacendero took care of his other women in Manila, another man came, fell in love with her, took care of her. She bore him children. Years later,can the hacendero return to claim her, saying "She's mine. I have the title to prove it"? What about the farmer who says: "I have lived with her and loved her, and she has borne my children"?

We thought that the church and perhaps even the court would rule in favor of the farmer, if it were a question of a woman. But apply that to the land, and there will be an outcry against "communist" ideas.

If it were a woman, no one would consider it unusual to ask her whom she would choose, whom she loved. Do we ever think of asking the land? If the land could speak, would we listen?

Later, socialist and feminist thought modified our analogy. Ownership seemed such a limited concept. The husband does not "own" his wife. The tiller does not really own the land. The wife is a peasant, too.

Marxist categories gave us more precise insights. Relations of production (including ownership of the means of production) match the development of the forces of production. The language was more scientific, and relieved us of questions that sought absolute and rigid answers. But if we want to continue conversing with peasants, our language has to be not only scientific, but also national (Filipino) and popular. How much of the religious categories we have to retain is difficult to fix precisely. But one thing is certain. We have to "confront vague ideas with clear images."

A third conversation took me back a hundred years. It centered on liturgy and the Eucharist.

Part of the usual FFF talk on the dignity of peasants was to tell them that without the peasants, the priest can not say mass. He would have no bread and wine to offer, for these are products of peasants. Whenever I said this, I felt some unease. No peasant put the question bluntly, but eventually I verbalized their silent reaction: "Bread and wine might be produced by peasants, but not in the Philippines. Why can't we offer our own produce -- rice, as *puto* or *bibingka* (rice cake), and native wine?".

I thought of stories my liturgy professor told in class. During World War II, missionaries in Indonesia got cut off from their mass supplies and went to all sorts of trouble to come up with the prescribed materials for mass. I thought of a possible blockade of the Philippines, or running out of foreign exchange. We wouldn't be able to import wheat or wine. Did that mean Christ couldn't be sacramentally present in the Philippines?

I turned to my liturgy professor. should it not be food and drink, not specifically bread and wine? He said there was some debate on this in Rome. Even the blubber of the Eskimo was discussed. But he cautioned me against hasty changes.

A voice spoke from the distant past. A hundred years ago, Fr. Jose Burgos wrote about a "eucharist of rice". At the very least, I told myself, there would be no problem of supplies. Peasant leaders used to ask me why only the priest drank wine. I said it was simple economics. I couldn't afford to buy enough wine for all of them. And yet I knew from history that Filipino religious rites involved liberal use of drink.

What difference rice and native wine would make. Instead of the mass being the priest's affair, since he bought the hosts and wine himself, peasant families could take turn preparing their offerings. I thought of the sharper symbolism of rice cakes we would share at mass. Surely no landlord who took an unfair share of the harvest could take communion. His actions automatically excommunicated him.

One Christmas season, a group of peasant sailed all the way from Davao to press for their land rights. We had mass that included trays of rice cakes and other offerings donated by sympathizers. I spoke about the breaking of the host. We break it because we are poor, and do not have enough. We must share the little we have. Another FFF leader added: "Even though there is not enough to satisfy all, no one will go without any share. We will not accept the principle that because there's not enough to satisfy all, a select few must have their fill, and the rest must wait for these few to create abundance for them."

IN 1969, the FFF and its youth allies staged a three-month picket at the Bureau of Lands to press for government action on a number of land cases. We even managed to force an entry into Malacañang Palace to meet President Marcos and have him designate a panel to act on the peasants' problems. There are many stories to tell and long conversations into the night from that picket.

One afternoon, another group of peasants gathered opposite our picket line. Their number steadily swelled to thousands. The Khi Rho and FFF marshalls cordoned us off, worried about infiltration. "They are MASAKA," whispered a marshall. MASAKA was tagged by the govenment as a left-influenced peasant organization.

A KM member who was visiting me at the picket (I knew her from way back and she even worked for a while with the FFF) was saddened by the marshalls' reaction. "We should not add to the peasants' divisions. Why can't we unite?" I asked her to walk with me through the other demonstration. I read their handouts, denouncing a semi-colonial and semi-feudal society, wondering what transformation radical language would have to undergo to be truly incarnate. If they knew me as a priest, there in their midst, would they welcome me? Or would they react to me as a suspected infiltrator? Little did I know then that I would have even longer conversations with them.

Late that night, a group of us exchanged impressions about the MASAKA demonstration. One of the peasant leaders from Laguna said something that shook us all. "I don't think we can solve the peasants' problems through pickets like this. I think it will need a revolution." One of the Khi Rho members blurted: "Have you been talking to the KM?" The FFF leader shook his head, refusing to be slighted. "You sent me on fact-finding teams," he said. "I thought only a few of us had problems. Now I know peasants all over the Philippines have problems."

He turned to me, his eyes intent on my face. "You have helped me see the need to organize and fight. Will you still be with us when we go beyond pickets and demonstrations?"

Perhaps it was because I knew he lived on the lake shore. Perhaps his challenge scared my mind into seeking shelter in familiar images.

But hearing him, I thought of him saying, "I will launch out into the deep", and the unspoken question: *Baka hanggang pier ka lamang* (Perhaps you won't go beyond the port).

I know I did not dare to answer that night. He did not press me and merely watched my half-smile fade. I thought his eyes were deeper than the lake, intense but quietly calm, like the lake's surface, giving no hint of a storm within.

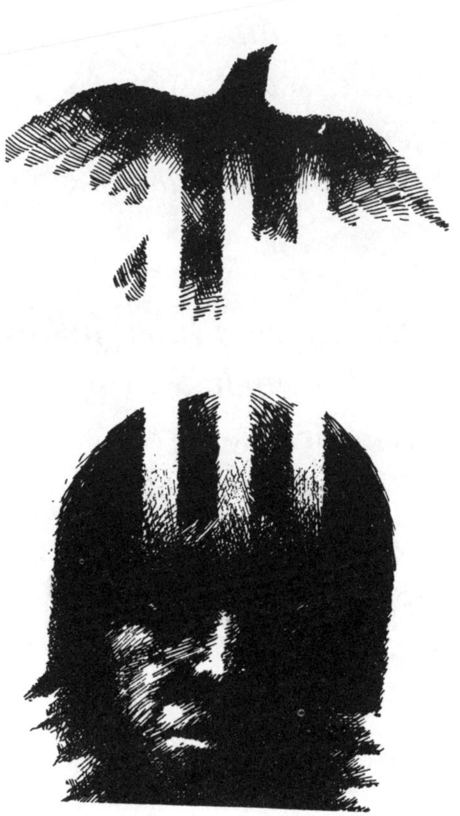

Section Two

through the storm

Wind, rain
Soak, scatter
seeds,
Roots must reach deepest.

Where trees have fallen
With clenched branches
We form a forest
Blooming green
Bursting red.

IN SEARCH OF A POLITICAL LINE

THE night of the "Battle of Mendiola", I was with a young couple who had asked me to officiate at their wedding the day after. On my way home from Manila to Quezon City, the jeepney I rode asked the passengers to get off. I walked through an alley and found myself in the middle of a street battle, just a block away from the bridge.

It wasn't much of a battle. The student protestors had only stones and some Molotov cocktails, one of which had set fire to a truck. The flames lit the faces of the students, but I couldn't recognize any. The military were dark, vague figures on the bridge.

Suddenly, I heard someone shout my name. Startled, I stepped back from the sidewalk, into the shadows. Then I saw the flushed faces of some UP freshmen I had met at a seminar the week before "*Rebolusyonaryo na rin kami!* " (We are now revolutionaries!). They took my hand and swept me along their forward rush.

We had advanced only a few meters when we heard the shooting, and the shouts: "*Takbo! Namamaril sila!* " (Run! They are firing!) We scampered to avoid the charge of the soldiers. A few blocks back, we clambered over the iron gate of a small chapel. When it seemed safe, we cautiously climbed out, and I continued my way home.

All I could think of was the wedding at which I was to preach the next morning. What should I say? I couldn't shake off the images and feelings from that unexpected encounter.

I preached on weddings and riots. How private feelings must seek public expression, like wedding vows and public protest. Then I was off to a farmers' meeting in Bulacan, where an FFF leader surprised me by using Mao's analogy of the egg, adding his personal twist. He said that an egg is best hatched from inside, when the chick breaks it with its beak. If the shell is broken from outside, the chick might not be ready to crawl out, or the opening might be at the wrong place. It would have to come out, back first. But if we leave it to the chick, the shell will be broken at the right time and the right place. I asked him where he picked up the idea. He said he was improving on what he heard from an FFF leader in Cavite.

THE First Quarter Storm of 1970 is justifiably celebrated as a historic event. But to those of us who worked with the FFF and whose center of gravity was in the provinces, it had limited immediate impact. The eye of the storm was in Metro Manila.

Unlike other Christians, we were not disturbed by the cries of "*Rebolusyon!* " or by the quotations from Mao. We had already read Mao on our own, especially his four articles: *On Contradiction, On Practice, On New Democracy* and *On The Chinese Revolution.* We picked up enough to realize that revolution calls for organization, especially of the main force, the peasants.

It was not till one year later that the peasants and students I worked with finally felt the full force of that First Quarter Storm. It was not just a storm, meant to shake the false peace of the existing (dis) order. Our roots in the peasants enabled us to weather that. It was also a sowing. It scattered seeds across the land, and by 1971, we realized that those seeds had lodged themselves deep in our consciousness and had struck roots in our practice.

The seeds sown during that storm were the elements of a general political line. In the technical language that we eventually got used to, the First Quarter Storm "broadcast on a nationwide scale the national democratic political line."

Slowly, we sorted out those elements. One was analysis, macro-analysis: What is the social formation of the Philippines? What

are the prevailing modes of production? A second, using class as the basic social category, answered the question: Who are for change? Who are against change? The third was about political strategy: How will the government be replaced by a better government? Finally, questions about alternatives: economic, political, cultural.

As originally broadcast, the national democratic political line went thus: The Philippines is semi-feudal and semi-colonial. The basic problems are imperialism, feudalism and bureaucrat capitalism. The target classes are the imperialists, landlords and comprador bourgeoisie. The motive forces are the workers (the leading force), the peasants (the main force), the petty bourgeoisie and the national bourgeoisie. The basic political strategy is a protracted people's war. The alternative is national democracy, whose perspective is socialism.

Like rice seeds, the elements of that political line were enclosed in husks. Sometimes we confused one for the other. Much of the language came from Marxism, from Mao. In technical terms, we couldn't clearly distinguish political line and ideology, national democracy and Maoism. Because of our emotional and intellectual blocks about Marxism, we found it difficult to accept the logic of national democracy.

Those who sowed the seeds were not always helpful. Although the national democratic line was formulated by the CPP, it was broadcast mainly by the student protestors. Some of them turned us off with their arrogant posturing as radicals. Feeling superior for having the "correct line," they looked down on those they considered reformists. I know of more than one "moderate" who took longer to adopt the national democratic line even when they were already convinced of its logic, simply because they knew that some radicals would make them feel as surrenderees, rather than welcome companions.

Later, in prison, I asked some CPP leaders about the First Quarter Storm, and the chaff that was mixed with the grain. One of them explained: "There were only 10 of us in Manila. The leadership we could exert was mainly to provide the line. Organizationally, the majority were on their own. They developed their

own methods and style of work." Even if they had been more numerous, he doubted if they could have avoided the shortcomings and mistakes of the radical student movement. "Growing up pains," he said.

It helped that literature started to multiply. We could read them in our own circles and at our own pace, without having to put up with the preachers who could have used some lessons in homiletics. There were also enough national democrats who engaged us in dialogue, rather than polemics. We learned to distinguish medium and message.

AMONG Christian activists, there were four types of response to that storm and the sowing.

The first group accepted the national democratic line, and joined the existing national democratic organizations. Most joined the legal organizations, like KM or the many groups that sprouted to form the Movement for a Democratic Philippines (MDP). A few joined the illegal organizations, the NPA in the countryside, or the unarmed cells of the urban underground.

Two friends in Khi Rho took this path. Soon after the First Quarter Storm, the Khi Rho leadership met in Laguna. There was heated debate on taking sides: either we are with the government, or with the demonstrators against government. The majority decided to "wait and see." There and then, my two friends resigned. They soon joined KM, but couldn't shake off a lingering suspicion for a long time. Five years later, I met one again, in prison. He had "gone to the hills", was wounded and captured.

A second group reacted to the storm and the sowing in an exactly opposite fashion. Opposed to revolution and to anything Marxist, they sought to come up with a comprehensive Christian alternative that eventually got baptized as social democracy. Although clearly reformist, they had to assert that they were radical, because of the temper of the times. Like many of us, they equated national democracy with Marxism, except that they rejected both.

A third response was represented by the SCM, when it renamed itself *Kilusang Kristiyano ng Kabataang Pilipino* (KKKP or 3KP)

in May 1971. Its leaders and members accepted the national democratic line, but maintained an independent organization that was explicitly Christian. They were not satisfied with the personal and private resolution that Christians in the secular ND organizations struggled to achieve. For many of these, it was enough to tell themselves that their original impulse to join was from their understanding of faith as an imperative to love.

Because SCM was explicitly Christian and institutionally related to the churches, it felt the need to justify its involvement in Christian, theological, terms. In the secular ND organizations, Christians were under pressure to show the relevance of their Christian categ ries, compared to nationalist and Marxist concepts. In the SCM, the opposite pressure existed. It had to prove that being a national democrat did not mean being Marxist, and that being revolutionary did not mean ceasing to be Christian.

It took the SCM more than a year of struggle to come up with a Christian rationale for its political option. They drew me into the process, forcing me to think through political theology (we had no inkling of "theology of liberation" yet) with them. Because of the blurred perception common to us then, national democracy and Marxism were both discussed. We asked not only about the "political incarnation" of our faith in national democracy. We also asked about faith and ideology.

Among the first Christian-Marxist encounter was our study of the *Five Golden Rays*, starting with Mao's speech "Serve the People" and the accompanying commentary. Hearing Mao speak about serving the people "wholeheartedly," and struggling against selfishness, the roots of ignorance and fear, I could only think of other biblical passages. I remember an SCM's spontaneous reaction: "We can get the same imperative from the Bible! " And almost immediately after: Why don't we hear that challenge from our church leaders? " It was almost inevitable that the main slogan of KKKP turned out to be: "Love your neighbor, Serve the People. Struggle for National Liberation and Democracy! "

The slogan represents the two linkages we made between Christianity and Marxism. One was political — "Struggle for national liberation and democracy." Christians and Marxists, both Filipinos, join in one political line. We called it revolutionary ecumenism. The other linkage was ideological, or, more accurately, ethical. We felt that the biblical commandment "Love your neighbor" and Mao's call to "Serve the People" both spoke to us of the truth we sought. Most of the KKKP were less bothered by theoretical concepts about God (they even complained that the "Kingdom of God" never became clear to them). What bothered them was the dedication, the total self-giving, that they felt Christians should consider an imperative of faith, in the same measure that their peers who called themselves Marxists dedicated themselves to the struggle.

Because of the Christian-Marxist dialogue, we learned to avoid a moralistic judgment on ourselves and others. While we recognized personal responsibility and decision, we also accepted the insight of social constraints, of class influence. We traced our hesitations not only to a less than faithful commitment to our faith, but also to our middle class origin and status. There was loose talk about "Christian-Maoists" or "Maoist-Christians." It is more precise to say that many of us wanted to be "proletarian Christians," having accepted the insight that as a social class, the proletariat's interests were more selfless.

THE fourth type of response took longest to make. It involved the biggest number of companions, those in Khi Rho and FFF. When the Khi Rho leadership "decided not to decide," they faithfully reflected the stance of their members and those of us who worked with the FFF. In fact, the peasants in the FFF served as our excuse to evade the theoretical challenge posed by the national democratic line. We had been drawn into the work, believing with the FFF leadership that "the peasants have the cause, but no voice; students have the voice, but no cause."

With that framework, it was easy to look at the storm as a passing outburst. Instead of paying attention to the seeds that were sown, we looked for our bearings in the growth of the peasants' consciousness. "Let the people (peasants) decide." Refusing to be labelled national democrats or social democrats, we considered ourselves neither radical nor moderate. In the pop language of later

activists, we were neither "nat dem" nor "soc dem," but "let dem."

Even our selective reading of Mao reinforced that position. Since he said that peasants and workers were the main and leading forces in the new democratic revolution, we were not impressed by the burgeoning student movement. We would have been more receptive of the national democratic line if it embodied itself in the classes we proclaimed ourselves as servants to. But the NPA and the revolutionary peasant movement were hardly present then outside the guerilla zone in Tarlac and Pampanga, and the urban workers' movement was not very visible to us.

We quoted with approval Mao's insistence on the "mass line." But we interpreted the slogan "from the masses, to the masses" one-sidedly, as if our politics should be a mere gathering and refining of the peasants' spontaneous consciousness. Not only did that deny us our right to develop our own consciousness. It also ignored the fact that the peasants (and workers) develop their consciousness, not in isolation from other influences, but in a dialectical process, involving their reflection on their immediate experiences and the ideas brought in "from outside." We were correct to insist that the "mass line" meant we should not expect things to change unless the masses are convinced and participate. Our mistake was in thinking that the masses should decide spontaneously, insulated as it were from "contamination."

We later learned to recognize ourselves in the critical language used to analyze political practice: "empiricist," "populist." Since the peasants we were in touch with did not articulate a comprehensive political line, we did not feel the need to, either. We were especially amused by those who tried to foist social democracy on us as *the* Christian alternative. Most of them, we felt, were more panicked by the spread of national democratic literature than anything else. We could show more sympathy if they engaged in some "mass work" with peasants and workers.

It was within our bias for "practice" and the peasants that the seeds of the national democratic line sprouted. Some FFF leaders in Batangas reported that they were brought at gunpoint to a cemetery, told to strip, and warned not to continue their work.

Some FFF members in Agusan were hung by their feet, while armed men interrogated them. Khi Rho and FFF members in Negros had to crawl at night to avoid being shot by a private army.

Questions started to come. Should we not prepare for the violence that our legal but militant organizing provoked? It was not revolution we were thinking of, just self-defense. Unlike the radicals who focused on state violence, and called for revolutionary violence against the state, our initial perception of violence was that coming from private armies, bodyguards and security forces of landlords and warlords.

I remember how tense and heated the debate was at a meeting of the FFF national council to which the national chaplains were invited. Should FFF leaders not arm themselves? To defend themselves from the landlords' hired guns? Other chapters did not wait for policy decisions from Manila. They did what they felt they needed to do.

By 1971, another question posed itself. Elections for local offices were to be held in November, together with elections for some Senate posts. The FFF was organizationally strong enough to endorse candidates. But the choices offered by the two-party system seemed equally undesirable, pro-landlord. Should the peasants not put up their own candidate?

Slowly, without benefit of Engels' or Lenin's writing on the state, both FFF and Khi Rho leaders and members looked beyond tenant-landlord relations, class to class relations, to the issue of political power. Actually, the self-image we had that we were still looking for a political line was only partly true. In practice, we acted within a reformist line. For example, after the Agrifina picket, the FFF and most of the Khi Rho supported the re-election bid of Marcos against Osmeña, in the 1969 presidential contest.

Bit by bit, branch by branch, the state revealed its essence to us. First to lose our trust was the judiciary. An FFF lawyer who won his fair share of agrarian cases in Luzon, found out that his legal skills were of little use in Davao. He admitted encouraging his peasant clients to resist the court's decisions, and got jailed him-

self for contempt of court. In Manila, FFF and Khi Rho leaders got jailed for occupying the Justice Ministry in protest over the lawyer's imprisonment. By the time martial law was declared, 70 agrarian cases filed by the FFF were unacted upon in one small province alone. One peasant member was so enraged by a judge's patent bias that he went amok. He was killed before he could reach the judge with his sickle.

The legislature, both Senate and Congress, were the focus of pressure in 1971, for a more effective land reform law. Some changes were made, but in the process of lobbying, the peasants and students literally felt the class bias of the "people's representatives."

The executive branch took longest to unmask, except at the local level. I think that part of the reason was we didn't think at all then of replacing government officials, especially at the national level, as the most important political change. We had an "anarchist" tendency, reflected in the FFF image of the government as a car, and the people as a driver. The car is organized, and if the people were also organized, the people would control the government as their servant. But if people were disorganized, like a drunken driver, the car would take them for a ride.

Following that thinking, we concerned ourselves with insuring that peasants were organized, so that whoever held office, whatever party held power, the people's organizations could check them. We looked with suspicion on anyone who ran for public office, no matter how he promised to be a different breed.

Soon, it was not just private armies and bodyguards that threatened the peasants. To their surprise, the government troops that they called in to mediate between the FFF and the landlord's men took the landlord's side.

WHEN did the pieces come together? When was the leap from perceptions to concepts, to judgment, to decision? How much influence did national democratic literature have in the process? It is difficult to tell. Like the seed growing unseen, experience sought explanation, and practice found the theory

that matched it. The signs were varied. Some would request me for certain books. Others asked probing questions. Still others gave advance notice that they might have to say goodbye, sometime later.

The leave-taking was very Filipino, long drawn out, with many words and also tender silence. What we wanted above all was that the bonds should not be broken, that decisions should not mean cutting off ties. We understood, with pain, the law of "uneven development."

When Khi Rho finally made the leap as a mass organization, we thought that the national democratic line would end our search for direction. To a great extent, it did. But questions still remained. What place is there for legal peasant struggles and organizations in a strategy that gives primacy to peasant guerilla war? What specific roles should Christians assume, within the division of labor among Christians and Marxists? What should we realistically expect from our churches?

Questions still remain. Some receive answers, only to provoke new questions. Together with KKKP, we realized that a political line is not only to be adopted and defended against competing lines. It is also to be developed, deepened and enriched as our practice advances. The seeds planted in our consciousness and experience will themselves produce new seeds. There will be many cycles of sowing and taking root, of growing to bear fruit, with seeds for another sowing. We received a line that is basically correct, but we have to do our share in adapting it, developing it, improving it. It is good seed, and it has taken root in the rich soil of our people who suffer and struggle. But it cannot remain seed. It must grow, drawing life from the soil, so that it can yield better seed for the next sowing.

THE CHALLENGE OF MAOISM AND THE FILIPINO CHRISTIAN

Lenten Lecture, 1971

MY thoughts on this topic are like Philippine society and the revolution: unfinished and fragmented. But we have to start with what we have; so here they are.

Maoism is so live a topic in the Philippines that like life itself it is rather complex and hard to define neatly. I have asked people what they mean by "the challenge of Maoism" and I have gotten various answers: (1) the People's Republic of China under Mao Tse Tung,* (2) the Communist Party of the Philippines (Maoist, 1968) and the New People's Army, (3) the ideology of Maoism, or more accurately, Mao Tse Tung Thought[1] (4) the programme for a people's democratic revolution,[2] and (5) the strategy and tactics of the national democratic organizations, especially the KM, SDK and MDP.

Petty bourgeois intellectuals, as a rule, focus on the "ideological challenge" and respond by frantically asking for a "counter-ideology" or a "Christian ideology." And as far as a I can gather, ideology means a mixture of philosophy and programmes. This attitude also leads to debates on revolution or reform, violence or non-violence, and similar topics, conducted in rather doctrinaire fashion and invoking the names of Mao and Christ in vain.

Since most of us in this crowd can be categorized as petty-bourgeois intellectuals, I will try to present the proper place of ideology in Maoism.

Note
***The People's Republic of China under Mao Tse Tung Section has been omitted.**

Maoism in the Philippines as the Challenge

The challenge of Maoism, therefore, to the Filipino Christian is not Maoism outside the Philippines but Maoism in the Philippines. But immediately, our bourgeois-intellectual bias asserts itself. It must be ideology, we say. I think not.

The first challenge is people — The Filipino Maoists, members of the Communist Party, the New People's Army, and cadres of the national united front organizations. It is the challenge of people who believe enough in something to devote their whole life and to be ready to die for it. Mr. Angel Baking speaks to PCC graduates of "revolution as a career." This passage from the *Programme for a People's Democratic Revolution in the Philippines* underlines this attitude:

> The Communist Party of the Philippines is determined to implement its general programme for a people's democratic revolution. All Filipino communists are ready to sacrifice their lives for the worthy cause of achieving a new type of democracy, of building a new Philippines that is genuinely and completely independent, democratic, united, just and prosperous. We are all keenly aware that the present bourgeois state and the reactionary classes that it serves will never surrender their political and economic power without a fight.[3]

My first impulse upon reading this paragraph was to scribble on the margin, "Moderates, where do you stand? " Unfortunately, among many of us, *moderate* defines not just political position or language but also commitment.

The second challenge is the party's programme of action :the concrete analysis of Philippine problems (historical and social), the analysis of the forces for revolution and reaction, the strategy and tactics of the national democratic revolution, and the outlines of the national democratic society. These may not be complete, but they are concrete. They refer us not to a system of thought or collection of principles, but to Philippine reality, problems and tasks.

By stressing people (*in* action) and programme (*of* action), I do not wish to minimize philosophy and ideology. I only want to

avoid the not-so-common attitude that treats Maoism as a philosophy (to be refuted as incomplete and inconsistent in classrooms).

Maoism is primarily a living movement, not a system of thought. It is method, not dogma.

Perhaps the sequence of Amado Guerrero's writings is significant: first, the founding of the party, then the programmes of action plus *Philippine Society and Revolution.* As of now, no direct philosophical topics. Philosophy is present, not as such but in its fruits: people and programmes. And he offers Philippine *Society and Revolution* only as a starting point for further inquiry into the Philippines, not as an end in itself.

Mao himself gives us the guidelines for properly appreciating his thought when he taught his cadres the proper attitude toward Marxism-Leninism:

> Our comrades must understand that we do not study Marxism-Leninism because it is pleasing to the eye, or because it has some mystical value, like the doctrine of the Taoist priests. . . . Marxism-Leninism has no beauty, nor has it any mystical value. It is only extremely useful. It seems that right up to the present quite a few have regarded Marxism-Leninism as a ready-made panacea; once you have it, you can cure all your ills with little effort. . . . Those who regard Marxism-Leninism as religious dogma show this type of blind ignorance. We must tell them openly, "Your dogma is of no use?" or to use an impolite formulation, "Your dogma is less useful than shit."(III, 43)

And earlier:

> The theories of Marx, Engels, Lenin, and Stalin can be applied to the whole universe. Their theories are not to be looked on as dogma but as a guide to action. We must study the viewpoint and method of its creators, with which they observed and solved problems. (II, 195)

Mao's Viewpoint and Methodology

Maoism should not be studied for its own sake alone, but used to study the Philippines. That is why the challenge of Maoism is the concrete Maoist movement in the Philippines and the concrete program of action in the Philippines, not Mao Tse Tung thought as such.

Listen to Mao again:

Can we claim to possess theoreticians just because we have read a great many books on Marxism-Leninism? No, we cannot say this. Marxism-Leninism is the theory that Marx, Engels, Lenin, and Stalin created on the basis of actual fact, and it consists of general conclusions derived from historical and revolutionary experience. If we have only read this theory but have not used it as a basis for research in China's historical and revolutionary actuality, have not created a theory in accordance with China's real necessities — a theory that is our own and of a specific nature, then it would be irresponsible to call ourselves Marxist theoreticians. . . .What type of theoreticians do we need? We need theoreticians who base their thinking on the standpoints, concepts and methods of Marx, Engels, Lenin, and Stalin, who are able to explain correctly the actual problems issuing from history and revolution, who are able to give a scientific interpretation and theoretical explanation of the various problems of Chinese economics, politics, military affairs, and culture. ((III, 37-38)

I cannot emphasize this enough, especially in the face of the "scriptural" treatment Maoism is getting both from government, pseudo-activists, and intellectuals. The important task is not to quote Mao verbatim but to study and change the Philippines using Mao's viewpoint and methodology.

But what are these? At the risk of doing injustice to the complex living thought of Mao, let me single out three main interrelated themes: (1) the unity of theory and practice (2) nationalism, and (3) revolution.

Unity of Theory and Practice

Discover the truth through practice, and again through practice verify and develop the truth. Start from perceptual knowledge and actively develop it into rational knowledge; then start from rational knowledge and actively guide revolutionary practice to change both the subjective and the objective world. Practice, knowledge, again practice, and again knowledge. This form repeats itself in endless cycles and with each cycle the content of practice and knowledge rises to a higher level. Such is the whole of the dialectical-materialist theory of the unity of knowing and doing. (I, 308)

This condensed Maoist epistemology is particularly important for any would-be ideologist. There is no challenging the need for ideology (Maoism itself is also an ideology) but we must be clear on the origin and purpose of ideology.

Where do correct ideas come from? They neither fall down from the sky nor spring from our inner being. They are the result of practice, social practice. For Mao, this practice is mainly the struggle for production and class struggle. He does not exclude political life, scientific and artistic pursuits, but he considers production and class struggle to be the major determinants of these other forms of social practice.

Of these other types of social practice, class struggle in particular, in all its various forms, exerts a profound influence on the development of man's knowledge. In class society, everyone lives as a member of a particular class, and every kind of thinking, without exception, is stamped with the brand of a class. (I, 196)

An ideology, therefore, to be valid, must be practical and partisan.

To call for a practical ideology is to demand that it arise from and be verified ultimately by direct experience. This is the basic reason why it is futile to formulate instant ideologies, why all ideologies are incomplete, and why ideologies formally arise from organized experience, especially, of a party.

The second meaning of *practical* is "changing reality according to the theory drawn from it." This describes not just the purpose of ideology, but even the full source of ideology; for Mao goes so

far as to say that it is only in changing reality that one gains full knowledge of it.

> If you want knowledge, you must take part in the practice of changing reality. If you want to know the taste of a pear, you must change the pear by eating it yourself... If you want to know the theory and methods of revolution, you must take part in revolution. (I, 300)

This unity between theory and practice is well-stressed by Mao especially for "armchair revolutionaries."

> The relation between Marxism-Leninism and the Chinese revolution is the same as between the arrow and the target. However, some comrades shoot arrows recklessly without a target. It is easy for them to harm the revolutionary cause. In addition, there are some comrades who merely take the arrow in hand, twist it back and forth, and say again and again in praise: "Excellent arrow! Excellent arrow!", but are never willing to shoot it. This type of person is a connoisseur of antiques who has hardly any relationship to the revolution. (III, 42)

To call for a partisan ideology is to recognize objective class divisions and to take sides with the "silenced majority," in order to articulate their side of the truth. This call for partisanship is generally the hardest to accept among petty-bourgeois intellectuals who prefer non-partisanship and who correspondingly conceive of abstract objective truth existing apart from particular objects and minds.

To sum up:

> The Marxist philosophy of dialectical materialism has two outstanding characteristics. One is its class nature: it openly avows that dialectical materialism is in the service of the proletariat. The other is its practicality; it emphasizes the dependence of theory on practice, emphasizes that theory is based on practice and in turn serves practice. The truth of any knowledge or theory is determined not by subjective feelings, but by objective results in social practice. Only social practice can be the criterion of truth. (I, 297)

This emphasis on practice and partisanship leads logically to what has been called the "Sinification of Marxism" by Mao.

Nationalism

> A communist is a Marxist internationalist, but Marxism must take on a national form before it can be applied. There is no such thing as abstract Marxism, but only concrete Marxism. What we call concrete Marxism is Marxism that has taken on a national form, that is, Marxism applied to the concrete struggle in the concrete conditions prevailing in China, and not Marxism abstractly used. If a Chinese communist, who is a part of the great Chinese people, bound to his people by his very flesh and blood, talks of Marxism apart from Chinese peculiarities, this Marxism is merely an empty abstraction. Consequently, the Sinification of Marxism — that is to say, making certain that in all of its manifestation it is imbued with Chinese peculiarities, using it according to these peculiarities — becomes a problem that must be understood by the whole Party without delay.[5]

This aspect of Maoism is often overlooked by commentators who claim that Asians will not accept Maoism because it is too Chinese. Some decades ago, similar commentators claimed that China would not turn Communist because communism is "foreign" and "Western."

The Communist Party of the Philippines, clearly recognizes its parallel task when it starts its preamble this way:

> The integration of the universal truth of Marxism-Leninism-Mao Tse Tung thought with the concrete practice of the Philippine Revolution is the supreme task of the Communist Party of the Philippines.[6]

Marxism-Leninism had to become Chinese in order to transform China. Similarly, Maoism must become Filipino if it is to be effective in the Philippines.

There is another meaning of the nationalism of Mao. It is the fact that his impulse to nationalism and revolution came before his full acceptance of Marxism-Leninism. These primary forces were directed and transformed by Marxism-Leninism, but they, in turn, transformed Marxism-Leninism into Maoism, the Asiatic synthesis.

This dynamic and original synthesis (indicated by the shift from "Mao Tse Tung's thought" to "Mao Tse Tung thought") can be observed by anyone who reads the unrevised writings of Mao chronologically. (Unfortunately, Maoism is being set up as scripture, leading many "Maoists" to quote Mao's writings out of

context, without reference to their origin.) And even if we do not take into account the Sino-Soviet split, we can still point to three significant results of the "Chinese pressure" on Marxism-Leninism.

(a) The role of the peasantry in the new democratic revolution.

Lenin had already realized that in underdeveloped countries, the peasants constitute the main force of the revolution but he always supposed that they would need the leadership of a proletarian party. Mao used to agree with such a traditional concept of the peasantry as a passive class, incapable of independent organized action, but his organizational work among them (social practice) convinced him that even the party could be born mainly from the peasants and the rural vagrants. His report on the peasant movement in Hunan contains this well-known passage:

> In a very short time, in China's central, southern, and northern provinces, several hundred million peasants will rise like a mighty storm, like a hurricane, a force so swift and violent that no power, however great, will be able to hold it back. (I, 23)

(b) The same basic source of theoretical advance (social practice) led Mao to give the national bourgeoise a longer-lasting role in the socialist construction of China.

(c) "The mass line."

Perhaps this style of speaking and working is one of the most dynamic aspects of Maoism. Listen:

> All correct leadership is necessarily from the masses to the masses. This means: take the ideas of the masses (scattered and unsystematic ideas) and concentrate them (through study, turn them into concentrated and systematic ideas), then go to the masses and propagate and explain these ideas until the masses embrace them as their own, hold fast to them and translate them into action, and test the correctness of these ideas in such action. Then once again concentrate ideas from the masses and once again go to the masses so that the ideas are persevered in and carried through. And so on, over and over again in an endless spiral, with the ideas becoming more correct, more vital and richer each time. (III, 119)

This "mass line" is part of Mao's tendency to trust the creative enthusiasm of the masses over organizational skill and technical

knowledge. This enthusiasm was the major factor behind the recent revolutionary movement within China against bureaucratization.

Revolution

There are innumerable principles of Marxism, but in the last analysis, they can all be surnamed up in one sentence: "To rebel is justified."[7]

Impatience with imperfect reality characterized Mao's earliest writings. Commenting on Bertrand Russell's lecture that socialism can be achieved by education instead of violence, Mao wrote:

My objections to Russell's viewpoint can be stated in a few words: "that is all very well as theory, but it is unfeasible in practice". . . If we use peaceful means to attain the goal of Communism, when will we finally achieve it? Let us assume that a century will be required, a century marked by the increasing groans of the proletariat. What position shall we adopt in the face of this situation? The proletariat is many times more numerous than the bourgeoisie; if we assume that the proletariat constitutes two-thirds of humanity, the one billion of the earth's 1,500,000,000 inhabitants are proletarians. . . who during this century will be cruelly exploited by the remaining third of capitalists. How can we bear this?[8]

Coupled with this impatience is a tendency to exalt the revolutionary will of man until it becomes not merely an important factor in history but an all-powerful force capable of re-shaping the material environment and even human beings themselves. This attitude is the result partly of his guerrilla experiences that led him to believe that men, not weapons, are the decisive factor in a revolutionary war. The same attitude underlies his contention that by changing their political attitudes men could change their objective class essence.

We can catch a bit of this spirit in Amado Guerrero's comment on population growth:

If the population were not subjected to foreign and feudal exploitation, not only could it become self-sufficient economically, but it could also excel in all fields of social endeavor. It could be a massive force for progress instead of being a "problem" interpreted in the Malthusian way by reactionaries who constantly prate about "overpopulation" to cover up the basic problems that are U.S. imperialism, feudalism, and bureaucrat capitalism.[9]

This revolutionary temper of Mao wishing to "subdue the earth" and transform man is more formally expressed in three theoretical developments of Maoism.

(a) *The concept of a permanent revolution*

For Mao, as for any Marxist, progress is achieved only by the resolution of internal contradictions. Life and progress are the result of struggle, and struggle is based on contradictions in every thing. Mao's contribution to this theory is not, as is commonly believed, the distinction between antagonistic and non-antagonistic contradictions, but his statement that there will always be contradictions even in the communist society; there will be no end to struggle.

(b) *The "poor and blank" theory.*

In traditional Marxism, the worker is considered the most revolutionary class, not only because he is oppressed, and therefore has the moral values of protest against injustice, but also because he has the technical skills for revolutionary leadership. That is why Marx thought of seizure by the proletariat of cities and factories in developed countries as the first stage of socialist revolutions. Correspondingly on the international Communist front, the Russians believe that the revolution by the underdeveloped countries should be directed by the Communist country with the most technical knowhow: Russia.

Mao's experience as a guerilla leader and his basic nationalism led him to make poverty and blankness virtues. Peasants are the most revolutionary precisely because they are blank, and therefore malleable; rural bases should be the first targets because they offer the best chances for building a radically new society; the seizure of cities is the last stage of the revolution. Internationally, China leads as the "poor and blank" socialist nation.

China's 600 million people have two remarkable peculiarities: they are, first of all, poor, and secondly, blank. That may seem like a bad thing, but it is really a good thing. Poor people want change, want to do things, want revolution. A clean sheet of paper has no blotches and so the newest and most beautiful words can be written on it.[10]

Mao's praise of "blankness" does not mean despising technical progress. It indicates an order of priorities. He prefers people who are both resolute and malleable. (One writer remarks that this reveals the strange mixture of humanist and totalitarian impulses in Mao.)

(c) *Moral incentives for building socialism.*

Mao rejects Stalin's "material incentives" for development of socialism. This attitude is perhaps more clearly expressed by Fidel Castro:

> We don't feel that the communist man can be developed by encouraging man's ambition, man's individualism, man's individual desires. If we are going to fail because we believe in man's ability, in his ability to improve, then we will fail; but we will never renounce our faith in mankind.[11]

With this we come a full cycle to where we started — people. Ultimately, Mao's message and challenge is people, transformed and transforming themselves and the earth.

Part Two: THE FILIPINO CHRISTIAN: GUIDELINES FOR PROPER RESPONSE

I thank whoever chose the title of my talk for using Filipino *Christian* instead of *Christianity* or *Church*. Not that I deny Maoism's challenge to Christianity or to the churches but simply because the ones who feel the challenge directly are the individual Filipino Christians who have responded more creatively to Philippine problems than any organized church as a whole.

Nilo Tayag's remark is to the point:

> It need not be the church as a particular institution but groups of Christians working with other radical movements who can undertake revolutionary changes.[12]

In line with the spirit of Maoism, I will not discuss Christian response immediately in academic and theoretical terms, basing myself on books and publications about Christian-Marxist dialogue abroad. I will try to present the reflections of Filipino Christians actually engaged in the struggle for national liberation in the Philippines.

What do I mean here by Filipino Christian? I mean somebody who considers himself *Filipino*, who is determined to stick it out in the Philippines and who has responded to the challenge of Philippine reality in one form or another. At the same time, he considers himself a *Christian*, with all the vagueness that accompanies the term, especially in relation to the nationalist struggle (a mixture of traditional belief in God and some philosophical, political and moral concepts).

The people I refer to arrived at their commitment in various ways. Some initially reacted to an overwhelming experience of the problem; some reached initially to a supposedly anti-Christian danger: Maoism. Still others found their commitment as a concrete direction of the enthusiasm they felt from Christiam renewal seminars. Whatever the origins of their initial commitment, they now share two basic impulses: an impulse to nationalism — to serve their countrymen — and in impulse to revolution — to serve

their countrymen by instituting radical structural changes in Philippine society.

The questions they ask are basically two: (1) We are nationalists; what is Christianity's role in nationalism? (2) We are Christians; what is our attitude toward Maoist nationalism?

The Christian Attitude Toward Nationalism

The first question is really the primary one, and it coincides with what commentators have written about Mao. Revolutionaries feel first the challenge of the situation as a nationalist challenge. Ideology and theology come later. Again, we need to stress what should be obvious: all seminars and talks on "theology of revolution," "political theology," and other current theologies make sense only to one who has started to act and have started to reflect on his actions. Theology as such does not breed commitment. At best it can remove hindrances to commitment.

One of the hindrances is the Filipino Christian's hesitation about explicit nationalist involvement. He realizes that personal acts of helping people who are suffering are not enough: that poverty and suffering are results of structures and systems best labeled as neo-colonial. Hence revolutionary nationalism (as distinguished from tradition-bound nationalism) is the concrete expression of love for promoting his brother's dignity. But "nationalism," even as a term, seems to be directly opposed to Christian "internationalism."

The "Christian nationalists" have found enough solid theological basis for their nationalism, especially the central doctrine of the Incarnation. "Christ is God-become-man, in order to save men. Don't talk therefore of Christianizing the Philippines. Talk first of Filipinizing Christianity. Christ must become Filipino if Filipinos are to be Christians." But the very fact that they have to prove what should be taken for granted reveals the major challenge of Maoism.

Can a Filipino Christian, as Christians, wholeheartedly and enthusiastically accept nationalism as Mao does instead of consider-

ing it reluctantly as a necessary but not desirable involvement? It seems that the colonial origins of Christianity in the Philippines and the continuing predominance of Western sources and writers prevent Christianity from being what it should be — incarnate, not in a Western people but in the Philippines.

The initial demands of such painful birth are parallel to Marxism-Leninism's Sinification: language and peasants (the main bearers of national consciousness).

But these are not enough. Nationalism, if it is to be an effective movement and not just a romantic recollection of an idealized, primitive past, must be mainly concerned with changing inadequate structures, leaders, and concepts — it must be revolutionary. But revolution calls for ideology.

THE CHRISTIAN ATTITUDE TOWARD MAOIST NATIONALISM

Now, Maoism, or more concretely, the national democratic movement, presents itself as the most vocal and concrete programme and ideology. What posture should the Christian nationalist adopt toward it? Does he have a Christian ideology? Is Christianity itself an ideology? Here, both historical experience and inadequate theological education have caused the Filipino Christian more than normal confusion.

In the past Christianity has been practically identified with certain systems and has become an ideology, a cultural captive and apologist either of feudalism or colonialism. (Perhaps, split-level Christianity is but a reflection of our semi-feudal and semi-colonial society.) Nationalist revolution, then, against the rulers of the old order is branded not just subversive but heretical (i.e., unchristian).

As a reaction to such political absolutism, many Christians swing to a-political liberalism. They refuse judgment (modestly claiming incompetence) on any socio-political system and worry mainly about private morality with some excursion into public life when individual or corporate religious privileges are threaened. But such seeming lack of judgment is really consent by

silence, as is evident in the rather righteous condemnation of an alternative system whether socialist or not as subversive and unchristian and atheistic.

Reacting against such inadequate presentation of Christian political involvement, Christian nationalists have arrived either formally or implicitly at what might be called a "political theology." Again, contrary to petty-bourgeois impressions, political theology does not give a programme or ideology; it simply frees people from false choices and gives guidelines for proper choices. What are its basic outlines?

1) Christianity is faith, not ideology. The Church is not a party. There is no such thing as *the* Christian system, *the* Christian party or programme, *the* Christian ideology or even *the* Christian organization.

2) Hence, the worst error a Christian can commit is to be satisfied with a system as to identify it with Christianity.

This was a "sin of commission" for many Christians in relation to feudalism. But its reverse — "sin of omission" (consent by silence) — is the more current fault in relation to liberal democracy.

3) What should be the proper attitude? The basic attitude of a Christian should be to be critical and dissatisfied with any system and to express it (making sure that criticism includes self-criticism because he, too, is part of the system). Here the theme of the pilgrim Church, never established, always on the way to the Kingdom, is very appropriate. This is the same attitude expressed by the 16 Bishops of the Third World when they wrote.

Nevertheless, throughout her historical pilgrimage on earth, the Church is in practice always tied to the political, social and economic system that in a given period, ensures the common good, or at least an ordered society. So much so that sometimes the Churches may seem to be fused with such a system, united as if in wedlock. But the Church has only one bridegroom, and that is Christ. She is in no way wedded to any system, least of all, to the "international imperialism of money" (*Populorum Progressio)*, any more than she once was to the monarchy and feudalism of the Ancient Regime, any more than she will be in the future to some form of socialism . . . . As soon as a system ceases to ensure the common good to the profit of some party in-

volved, the Church must not merely condemn such injustice, but dissociate herself from the system of privilege, ready to collaborate with another that is better adapted to the needs of the time, and more just.[13]

Here, the Filipino Christian faces the Maoist challenge again. How critical has he been of the present system? How concrete and analytic has been his criticism? How vigorous and passionate has been his indictment of the present injustices? Certainly Maoist nationalists can hardly be accused of consent by silence.

The record of the organized Churches is even more pathetic. We have selective protest which comes a bit late and moderately. Christ's driving the moneylenders from the temple or John the Baptist's protest against Herod would be branded "imprudent" today.

4) But is criticism enough? No. One must also choose alternatives. Here the question comes again. How should a Christian choose? From among what choices? What would be the basis for his choice?

a) The Christian must make a political choice. He cannot take refuge in a "moral" pronouncement that has no political effectivity.

b) But he must not take the name of God in vain. He cannot simply brand one choice "unchristian" or promote the other as "Christian". This calls for the basic critical posture that I described above. All his choices can only be provisional, not absolute.

The basis of his choice of a programme, party or system, cannot be authority or terminology. "The Pope says so" or "Mao said that" cannot be the primary basis for choice. Love seeking to promote the greatest dignity of men should be his main guiding principle.

c) But to make this principle concrete, he must examine the different proposals of science and ideologies. What economic system, what political system, what methods? Here he must examine all proposals and choose (with the possibility of error) that which the

majority would understand and accept as promoting human dignity. Maoism and the national democratic programme is one of such proposals.

We can say therefore that under concrete Philippine conditions a Filipino Christian cannot make a Christian political choice if he does not seriously examine the challenge of Maoism, not just as a stimulus to dedication or as a co-critic of society, but even more, as a concrete proposal for showing effective love to his fellow-Filipinos.

For in the final analysis, to take the challenge of Maoism seriously is to take Incarnation in Philippine society seriously; to concretely analyze concrete conditions and to side with the oppressed people in their struggle for liberation, not as a self-appointed leader but as a servant of the revolution.

CHRISTIANS IN THE STRUGGLE FOR NATIONAL LIBERATION MAY 1971

It is evident by now that any meaningful fight for national liberation is basically a struggle against the ungodly trinity of systems — imperialism, feudalism and bureaucrat capitalism — systems which stifle the liberation of productive forces, both natural and human, in our society. But there are some aspects of the struggle that I would like to emphasize.

First of all, the long and arduous struggle is a historical process characterized by the unceasing dynamism of social forces. It is already there moving forward, often without the direct consciousness and decision of many of us. Hence, the struggle. First, to understand and analyze the forces that work for change or against change. Secondly, the struggle to hasten and heighten people's conscious participation in the struggle (together with this is the struggle to awaken others into realizing the need to recognize and to participate). And thirdly, to fight the forces of reaction.

This threefold struggle is even more difficult because it is uneven. The forces of imperialism, feudalism and bureaucrat capitalism have penetrated into our society in different degrees and the forces for change have likewise developed unevenly. This results in confusion and, sometimes, unnecessary revision. Some forces are more advanced in their consciousness and have total view of all targets and tasks. Other lag behind at least in some respects; they might struggle to liquidate feudalism, but not relate it to the anti-imperialist fight. Others might overlook the possibility of setbacks and mistakes, the need for flexibility and the need for a real united front. Unity in struggle (not uniformity) is a real task for all of us.

Faced with this struggle, we ask ourselves as Christians: Where do we stand? We cannot have the luxury of indecision. We either make choices or they will be made for us.

I'm glad that the question is asked of Christians, and not of Christianity. This prevents us from becoming too abstract, ideologically or theologically.

If we look at Christians in the Philippines, we see that they respond to the challenge in different ways and for different motives. The first question then, that I'd like to resolve is the proper motivation for participation in the struggle. Why are we in this, we who claim to be struggling together?

From contact with involved Christians, I see four possible reasons. Three are inadequate, though powerful. Only the last is authentic.

The first is reaction to social unrest, in the name of peace and order. We cannot deny that if the contradictions in Philippine society did not break out into social unrest, we cannot deny that many of us would not have felt the need to directly participate in the struggle and to analyze in a more sophisticated manner our participation in the struggle. We cannot deny that Christians are most active where people are already most visibly expressing their discontent, not just in words but in anti-social behavior: rallies, armed struggle, whether simple banditry or revolutionary guerilla war. We cannot deny that were it not for the vocal protests of many Filipinos, the demonstrations and the state violence, the uncertainty, the change in the normal rhythm of social life, most Christians would have remained passive or peripherally interested in the struggle for national liberation. But the danger with such motivation is this — many Christians value the re-establishment of peace and order so much so that they might accept a reactionary solution, suppression of revolutionary forces or probes into the causes of unrest that leave some people satisfied they have solved the problem simply because they have analyzed it.

The second motivation that is even more powerful and often goes together with social unrest is anti-communism. The explicit presence of Maoist language and the supposedly overwhelming strength of communist conspiracy have led many Christians to a special type of reactionary and competitive involvement. (More will be said about this later.)

A third and dangerous motive: the fear of irrelevance and the struggle to be relevant again. Churches and Christians feel the frantic need to update themselves, to get involved, for fear that the youth might leave them behind, that they might be left out of the mainstream (and public notice). They want Christianity and Christians to participate in the struggle, not so much because they believe Christians can do much for the struggle, but because the struggle can do much for Christianity. The motive is not so much to serve the Filipino people, but to serve (or preserve) Christianity by proving that it is not so irrelevant. This is a question that we must keep asking and answering: Do we insist so vehemently with so much passion sometimes, on the need for Christians and Christianity to be explicitly present in the struggle because we really believe them to be forces that can serve or is it because we want to save Christianity which we value? Do we need to involve ministers and priests because we need them or because they need us?

I think that we cannot completely purify ourselves of all traces of inadequate motives. But we must explicitly and emphatically concentrate on the most acceptable and most Christian motivation that the Bible presents to us — the programmatic announcement of Christ: "*The kingdom of God is at hand, repent.*"

The Kingdom of God is at hand. The process of change to a more human and just society has long started. We must recognize it as basically a valid movement, even if it speaks in strange tongues.

Repent. Turn back on a crumbling old order out of which we are being called like Abraham. Struggle to create a new order in which Filipinos can grow into a more fully human people. To turn back is not to passively save ourselves but to actively destroy in order to liberate others.

Christians must acknowledge (with repentance) the earlier, more radical and more generous response of many Filipinos to these two-fold tasks. These people who have responded much ahead, much faster, with little hesitation, should cause us to feel shame — the first and minimum revolutionary emotion. If we cannot join for any other reason, let us struggle because we are ashamed of our inaction. Shame is a revolutionary emotion because it prevents us from yielding to the occupational hazard of Christians — to expect applause once we decide to participate. We

like to believe that the struggle will not succeed unless Christians participate; when we announce our decision to join we expect applause instead of the reproach: "*Bakit ngayon lang?* " (Why only now?)

Shame should also prevent us from immediately claiming a special place for Christians in the revolution and from immediately looking for leadership roles. To be ashamed of being late can lead us to accept humble roles, even anonymity in the struggle. We have to accept the same basic tasks: to expose and oppose oppression and to build revolutionary forces whether explicitly Christian or not.

But we gather these days because we believe we can still ask the question: After accepting humbly our common basic tasks in the struggle, do we have specific tasks as Chistians in the struggle for national democracy? I think we have.

The first concerns the analysis of the problem — Christianity as part of the problem. People who are at work have overcome an initial simplistic and romantic idea of the revolution and are accepting a multi-front, uneven, and protracted struggle. They also realize that forces of reaction have become more sophisticated. The establishment does not always directly suppress movements. It promotes deviations in the guise of revolutionary change. It diffuses revolutionary emotions by accommodations. Here, Christians have the specific task to expose and oppose the particular roles churches play in opposing revolutionary change.

This calls for concrete analysis of the churches as organized economic and political forces for reaction. Who can expose the specific roles the churches play in the economic life of the Philippines, the collusion of their leaders with the powers that be, the relationships between missionaries and their mother churches in imperialism? Who have access to facts? Who can expose the church-owned schools and their programs for suppressing student dissent, for channeling potentially revolutionary forces into reformist activism? These problems can be attacked from outside even by those who do not belong to the churches; but much of it can be dismissed as biased and based on incorrect information. What if members give the inside stories?

Secondly, Christianity as opium, a mystifying cultural force. Here we must pay special attention to a possible deviation. We can expect valid and effective criticism of Christianity as an overtly feudal and colonial culture. But this might lead to a transformation into capitalist Christianity, a seemingly more progressive version, symbolized by the religious order in relation to the diocese, or more accurately, by a Filipinized religious order as opposed to a foreign-led religious order, still capitalist, still reactionary, still bourgeois. Here we have to insist radically on formulating our criticism of Christianity as culture and expressing our counter-consciousness in the Filipino language. Otherwise, we might unwittingly be influenced by the radical theological literature from Europe and America which hide a reformist political content inside a radical theological language. For us to liberate Christianity from colonial and feudal captivity, we must liberate the *Word* from foreign words and incarnate it in new words that we will forge in the heart of the struggle. What new theological language will arise, how much will come from Marxism-Leninism-Mao Tse Tung Thought as applied to the Philippines, I do not know. But I think we can only liberate Christianity in the struggle for national liberation if we can struggle to formulate our reflections in our own tongue, even if it is still less precise. There is no short-cut. We cannot be satisfied with reprinting, collecting, editing and reinterpreting radical writings from other lands.

Together with these two problems is the problem of clerico-fascism. Again, we have to analyze a more sophisticated version of clerico-fascism in the Philippines. It is not the classical fight for blatant privileges of the churches or direct political control.

I think it will be more subtle. The social base will not be feudalism but agricultural capitalism in the form of integrated rice complexes or cooperative plantations. Cooperative, not in the revolutionary sense of class operatives but bourgeois cooperatives that involve different classes who seem to have equal votes and control and yet are controlled by the board of directors who have sophisticated management training. In industry, it will be the junior partners of multi-national firms and the labor unions that have practically become junior partners of management. In politics, it is the particular sector that is most enthusiastic about the Constitutional Convention — the out-of-power petty bourgeoisie. It is petty,

but still bourgeois. There could be opposition to direct American domination, but not to some partnership with Japan or more probably with Germany (our growing third partner in trade). Indications of this is the seemingly nonvested financing being given by German foundations for labor education and bourgeois cooperatives in the Philippines;

Apart from channeling anti-feudal and anti-imperialist forces into "junior capitalism," two aspects of this modern form of clerico-fascism are particularly harmful. One is the divisive influence of the proposed baptism of social democracy as the Christian choice. The other is selective protest (consent-by-silence) of the churches. When the state suppresses democratic dissent involving national democratic movements, churches are either silent or even secretly relieved. They protest against state violence only when it involves "moderate" groups. In some cases, there is even direct collusion to stifle other forms of dissent, in the name of anti-communism.

The second specific task of Christians in the national democratic struggle is to rediscover the liberating message and power of Christianity.

This is not something we can simply take for granted. Too many Christians complacently think that Christianity is automatically considered as liberation. We have to prove this in the struggle both against those who wish to make it a domesticating approval of the status quo and those who have legitimate reservations about the truth of what we preach. But this task is necessary if we want to hasten the mobilization of the masses, for we cannot deny that Christian consciousness (no matter how inadequate) acts as a block to their revolutionary decision.

This is why we have to consider seriously the liberation of our liturgy and our churches in general. More often than not, we simply have to denounce our churches as whited sepulchers and empty tombs from which the spirit has departed — irrelevant relics of an old older. But we also have the task to build a "Peoples' Church" to help organize radical Christians and to launch a cultural revolution within our theology and our churches.

Against the divisive tactics of clerico-fascism, we propose a revolutionary ecumenism that cuts across traditional sectarian religious affiliations, exposes the false divisions promoted by the churches and establishes basic unity in the struggle among Christians of different denominations. This ecumenism is even more directly concerned with our struggle for unity, and unity through struggle, with the non-christians, the Muslims, cultural minorities and the Marxists.

This last point is a crucial question for Christians in the national liberation movement. We cannot challenge the fact that Marxism and Marxists play the leading role in the struggle for national democracy. We cannot deny either that many Christians experience hesitation and confusion about their relationship to Marxism and the Marxists.

I do not propose to answer this question completely. I only want to establish the basic premises for our answer and propose a posture that I think Christians should adopt.

The first premise is again the programmatic message of Christ, the kingdom of peace, freedom, justice and love. A Christian whose vision is not blurred by his hard-heartedness can only adopt a basically critical attitude toward any system in which he lives. And here is his first point of agreement and cooperation with the Marxists: *common criticism of an unjust society.*

All systems must be judged imperfect against the perfection of the kingdom which is being realized wherever men struggle against dehumanization. To baptize one particular choice "Christian" simply because it speaks in "Christian" terms and counts Christians in its ranks is theological prostitution.

But to say that a Christian is free from absolute choice is not to allow him to abdicate choice. He must choose (with the risks of any decision) the system and methods that he believes most likely to promote human dignity at any given stage of history and society.

Some Christian organizations have chosen the national democratic programme as their Christian commitment to national libera-

tion.[7] What can they say to those who would accuse them of being unwitting or, at best, naive tools of an ideology and leadership that other Christians sanctimoniously condemn as atheistic?

As a posture from which to answer, I propose that we Christians adopt as our title: *SERVANT OF THE REVOLUTION*.

This is, first of all, a recognition of our inadequacy and our duty to learn not only from the masses but also from the Marxists. For our Christianity does not give us political and economic categories and other scientific tools to correctly analyze and solve the contradictions in our society. It is also the recognition that others have "mastered" this task ahead of us and have the wisdom that only direct and organized experience in the struggle can give.

But servant of the revolution? Why not servant of God? Or even servant of the people? Apart from being an explicitly dynamic concept (avoiding the danger of a static concept of God and people), revolution is conveniently ambiguous. A Christian can interpret it as God at work in the world, breaking up the old and creating the new. A humanist can look at it as a people emerging from their submerged status in a "culture of silence" into power and dignity. The Christian does not presume to have led or initiated the process. He can only recognize and promote it, and criticize deviations.

To be a servant of the revolution is to recognize the leadership of others in the revolutionary process without being servile (abdicating criticism) and without being a servant of any ideology. Ideology serves the revolution, not vice-versa.

The revolution is bigger and more creative than our inadequate attempts to categorize it. It is life. We Christians can hope that in serving the struggle with "strange men speaking in strange tongues," we will find meaning in the paradoxes of our faith.

"HE WHO IS WILLING TO LOSE HIS LIFE WILL FIND IT.
HE WHO WISHES TO LEAD MUST SERVE."

THE PASSION, DEATH AND RESURRECTION OF THE PETTY-BOURGEOIS CHRISTIAN 1972

In the beginning was the first quarter storm of 1970 and the annunciation of the birth of a new Filipino — anti-imperialist, anti-feudal, and anti-bureaucrat capitalist. Like all births it was rather noisy and bloody. The child's new cry was loud and angry and repeated regularly, and he spoke in strange tongues.

The high priests and elders were afraid and wondered who this child was. Was he the illegitimate grandson of Mao Tse-tung, *anak sa labas*, result of seduction and infiltration? Was he the son of Jose Maria Sison? The child claimed legitimate continuity with Bonifacio and included Lapu-Lapu in his genealogy and wanted recognition as the first fruit of nine years' struggle in the dark womb of the sixties, the product of the multiplication and organization of the first scattered cells for study and action. The elders asked the wise men of Congress to appoint a committee and received a 500-page volume enumerating all possible causes excluding the high priests, elders and wise men. So they decided to name him "Maoist" and ordered the soldiers to massacre every newborn child of that generation.

And so it came to pass that the children had to remain in exile, go underground, or climb the hills from where salvation comes.

There were also Christians who watched the scene but didn't quite remember their own parallel beginnings. Instead they had memories of Ramon, the messiah who delivered them from the Huks, consecrated them to the Sacred Heart of Jesus, and commended them to the protection of Uncle Sam; but who died and didn't quite rise again in the succeeding saviors of the people: Carlos who preached the gospel of Filipino First, Diosdado who announced the coming of a new era, and Ferdinand whose wife circumnavigated the globe to make our nation great again. So they turned to Raul who told them to stay securely inside their home and bolt the doors and windows as did the Christians before Pentecost and await his revelations on their TV screens.

And so it came to pass that these Christians held seminars and group discussions and kept off the streets to avoid confusing the

soldiers who, after all, were only after those who spoke in strange tongues that had to be Chinese because they were anti-American.

And there were also those Christians who watched their flocks in the field, leaders and lawyers of trade unions and peasant land reform groups, socially-oriented youth volunteers, liturgical drop-outs who communed with the masses rather than at mass. They had long been struggling in the even darker womb of the Church against the lightning and thunder of episcopal anathemas and ecclesiastical intrigue. The First Quarter Storm disturbed and threatened to disperse their flock which they had painstakingly organized in the face of civil and ecclesiastical hostility.

And so it came to pass that a lot of questions arose among Christians. Is imperialism the principal contradiction to Philippine nationalism? Are peaceful reforms only deviations from the correct path of protracted armed struggle? Is there no middle ground between a worsening status quo and a threatening national democratic revolution? Is there a Christian ideology, the papal encyclicals perhaps? Is there a Filipino ideology? An ideology for the Third World? Other Christians, especially those engaged in direct organizational work among peasants and workers said: "Stop this premature search for an ideology! Let us first integrate with the peasants and workers, organize them and synthesize with them our political line and ideology."

But the need for a more systematic and scientific style of work and the ferment generated by the First Quarter Storm forced everyone to seriously struggle with the ideas and theories proposed in numerous mimeographed and printed articles, pamphlets, books, speeches: Jose Maria Sison's *Struggle for National Democracy;* Renato Constantino's writing; Montemayor's two books and speeches; Amado Guerrero's *Philippine Society and Revolution* and pamphlets: Freire's *Pedagogy of the Oppressed;* Alinsky; Mao's *Red Book*, *Five Golden Rays*, *Selected Works;* Che Guevara; Latin American theologians, and thousands of mimeographed and transcribed speeches, summaries, outlines, comments, and reprints during social action, social orientation, social awareness seminars, teach-ins, etc.

By the year's end, there were quite a number of organizations identified as Christian, as "moderates," as opposed to the "radicals."

These were the labor and peasant unions like FFW and FFF, youth organizations like Khi Rho, Kasapi, Lakasdiwa, YCSP, KASK, NUSP (by association), even a would-be political party that couldn't make up its mind like CSM. Quite a few priests, ministers, nuns and seminarians were in organizational work, apart from the different projects of the Social Action Centers. But among their ranks and leadership, a definite split was developing on the question of radicalism and relationship to the national democratic mass organizations. One wing was definitely for reformism, for changes within the system but not of the system, and correspondingly looked with hostility at the national democratic groups. One of the youth members symbolized this when he sheepishly confided, "I used to rejoice secretly whenever a KM got arrested or killed. "*Ngayon, parang namamatayan na rin ako.*" The other wing arrived through theory and practice at the conviction that radical change of the system is necessary. It was willing to learn from the systematic literature and experience of the national democratic groups.

This led to another theological and ideological struggle. Does Christianity provide a unified guide to social involvement? Are the social principles of the papal encyclicals binding and normative? Is there a Christian way of changing society? The answers came rather clearly from "political theology."

The normative character of the encyclicals and Christianity is negative. A Christian is supposed to be basically critical of any social system, because he believes that the destiny of mankind is the Kingdom, the perfect society of love, freedom, justice and peace. But to be basically critical of all social systems and to avoid identifying Christianity with any system doesn't mean not having to choose "provisionally, but not arbitrarily" the system and methods that promote humanization and liberation at a given historical stage of a given country.

What happens when two groups of Christians make provisional choices that are opposed to each other?

In May, 1971, the Student Christian Movement, an ecumenical organization of Christian youth, officially adopted the nation-

al democratic political line and joined the MDP, the national alliance of national democratic mass organizations.

By December 1971, Kilusang Khi Rho ng Pilipinas decided to adopt the national democratic formulation of national problems and solutions as its provisional basis for future ideological, political, and organizational work.

On February 17, 1972, a group of priests, pastors, nuns and seminarians formed the CNL, Christians for National Liberation, as a vehicle for open and organized participation in the national democratic cultural revolution. Other youth groups like the Methodist Youth Fellowship, the Student Catholic Action, the Kilusang Pambansa ng Kabataan (IFI), the Lutheran Youth Fellowship, and nameless study groups of seminarians and nuns are presently exploring their participation along the same lines.

There had always been Christians who had accepted the national democratic program. A survey of KM and SDK activists by some theology students revealed that 67 out of 85 respondents considered their work Christian, because it showed concrete love for poor. One is reminded of the KKKP (Kilusang Kristiyano ng Kabataang Pilipino, the Pilipino name of SCM) slogan: Love your neighbor. Serve the people. But they had always been considered radical *despite* their being Christian. But for SCM, its Christianity is precisely incarnate in the national democratic struggle.

Other Christian groups chose otherwise. They either rooted themselves systematically in the papal encyclicals and the Christian Democratic tradition of Europe and Latin America, or tried to synthesize from many traditions a Filipino, or Christian, or Third World ideology which they named social democracy or, more recently, democratic socialism. Still others preferred not to operate with a systematic ideology. Some members of these groups call SCM, Khi Rho and other similar groups "Communist fronts" (an accusation levelled by Marcos and the military at the KM, SDK, and other MDP affiliates). Sometimes, they more charitably brand them as unwitting and naive tools of a godless and materialistic ideology.

But the majority of Christians in both social democratic and national democratic organizations are not really concerned about who is more Christian or not. They are not even immediately worried about the precise relationship between Christianity and Mao Tse-tung Thought, even though this is an intellectually titillating topic. They know that Maoism directly or indirectly influences all groups, some more systematically than the others. Their common task is how to achieve in the most scientific way the liberation of the Philippines from the domination and exploitation of the imperialists and their native allies.

It is precisely this commitment to liberation that excludes any liberalism toward each other and toward their Christian faith. It is not enough to say. "You are sincere, *OK ka lang, may ginagawa ka naman e, di tulad ng marami d'yan.*" One must struggle to arrive at the most precise analysis, the most correct strategy and tactics, to learn the most from mistakes. And one must dare to ask the question: "Does Christianity contribute to national liberation? "*Hirap kasi, Kristiyano pa tayo!* " (It is difficult because we are still Christians!) exclaims an activist during a discussion on revolutionary violence and love.

Dale Noval, Khi Rho national chairman, describes the shift in emphasis: "Before, we tried to justify nationalism and revolution to Christianity. Now we have to justify Christianity to nationalism and revolution." And this "justification" of Christianity is not to make it palatable to the revolution so that it can be preserved. It is to try to define how (if at all) it can best serve liberation.

And for an activist whose interest is liberation at all costs, the ideological and theological question of Christianity's role becomes a very personal life-and-death question: "Am I still Christian? Do I want to remain Christian?". A girl who has been an activist for six months muses: "I got into the national democratic movement because I believe that to be a Christian is to serve the people. Now I am all caught up in analysis and political tasks and ideological education. And when my faith rises from gut level to my head, it comes in conflict with so many political and ideological ideas I consider correct. So I just keep my faith as basic inspiration. It doesn't clarify any of my political questions."

Sometimes there is an initial political answer. Since we are waging a cultural revolution, we have to start with the existing consciousness of Filipinos. They consider themselves Christians; to them, revolution and Maoism equal atheism equals loss of freedom to worship equals anything is better than that. Hence it is objectively advantageous to the national democratic movement if revolution is seen as a Christian imperative.

But one immediately realizes that this is wishful thinking, at least for the present, since the Christians who are for revolution are not considered the primary orthodox representatives of Christianity. Official and hierarchical Christianity is still on the side of the Establishment, either as a defense against subversion (communist witch-hunts) or as a weak sacristan-confessor. "For your penance, part with a little of what you stole, so that they don't take everything away from you." Besides, that would give only a tactical value to being Christian.

Hence the ever-recurring question: "What is the role of Christians in the struggle for national liberation?" Nelin Sta. Romana, national chairman of KKKP, formulated it differently: "The Christian Dilemma." How does one honestly claim to be Christian while choosing to work along lines that are rejected by other Christians as "atheistic, materialistic, and violent?"

Both questions still reveal triumphalist tendencies. The Christian is considered automatically qualified to be part of national liberation. Not only that, he is even supposed to have a special role. And if the other aspects of the movement cannot be reconciled with his faith, he would rather let the people remain as they are rather than violate his principles.

To combat this unchristian superiority complex we emphasized the call to repentance, a very basic biblical theme. Christians should continually be self-critical and should even be ashamed that others have participated in the struggle for national liberation much more resolutely and with greater sacrifice. But it didn't seem to be enough.

The other youth organizations in the MDP helped us find the answer. They had also been trying to define the role of youth as

youth, perhaps partly because of the cliche from Rizal's works: "Youth is the hope of the fatherland." Then they realized that roles are determined principally by class analysis. Hence their decision to engage principally in cultural revolution. Why? Because they are petty-bourgeois.

Suddenly, our feet were on solid ground again. We had started up in the air, with consciousness, rather than social conditions. We started with the term "Christian" and got confused, since we could not even be sure that it meant one and the same for a Christian landlord, a Christian tenant, a Christian capitalist, a Christian worker, a Christian Metrocom or a Christian NPA.

We forgot the principal scandal and good news of Christ, "a man in everything except sin." No wonder we were like Pharisees. "We thank you, God, that we are not like the rest of men. We are not subject to class analysis. We are not affected by class interests. We are moved only by theology and ideas. We only need to be informed about the issues and we will immediately act in favor of the poor." This is the meaning of repentance; to admit with the publicans. "Have mercy on us O Lord, we are sinners. We are petty bourgeois."

We are both petty and bourgeois.

Why sinners? Because we had unwittingly given proof of the radicals' complaint that Christians obscure class divisions and preach class reconciliation (Alinsky: "Reconciliation means I am in power and you get reconciled to it"). Of course even the radicals themselves do not always practice class analysis. They mistrust all actions of the PBSP (Philippine Business for Social Progress) and NFSP (National Federation of Sugar Planters) because their membership is capitalist and hacendero, yet they would still appeal to Cardinal Santos and other bishops, not realizing that they are not only church officials (and presumably acquainted with Vatican II and the encyclicals) but also landlords and capitalists.

Why sinners? Because we had thought of Christianity as a middle class, petty-bourgeois cross. We thought we were witnessing

the class struggle between exploiters and exploited from a non-partisan, as yet uncommitted, middle-class ground. Hence we could postpone our optional involvement while we hesitated and carefully weighed the consequences of our decision. Hamlets, soliloquizing "To be or not to be." But we were already partisan, bourgeois, no matter how petty. We were the servant class of the upper class.

Ideologically, we thought that we could find a middle-class mean between bourgeois capitalism and proletarian socialism and called it Christianity. Yet it was still bourgeois, except for its pettiness. And our middle-class position prevented us from immediately helping the proletariat, because we thought their style of collective action was Maoist while our concern for manageable personal groups was Christian.

And the mistakes that accompanied their collective acts made us draw back and postpone commitment, while waiting for a pure, sinless revolution. So we crucified ourselves on a cross of our own making, wanting to love, to serve the people, but always holding back because we might be used, because it might violate our principles, and so we loved "pure and chaste from afar." Virgins who loved too wisely but not too well, afraid to risk, waiting for immaculate conceptions and virgin births of plans, organizations, movements, societies.

It is terrible to realize how human one is. How painfully cutting the criticism against the petty bourgeois: "Characteristically subjective, individualistic, impetuous or easily cowed. . . careerist, given to anarchist organizing. . . vacillating, opportunist" (Amado Guerrero). Yet, like all revelation, it is liberating. The truth always sets one free, if only from ignorance about one's own captivity. Instead of trying hard therefore to lead the struggle for liberation and suffering the numerous vacillations and hesitations and fears that the petty bourgeois is heir to *(magulo ang isip, mahina ang tuhod)*, he frees himself from impossible dreams and fulfills his historic role of serving the peasants and the workers, the main and leading forces of liberation. The Christian in him is also liberated from the vain task of finding a distinctively, neither bourgeois nor proletarian, Christian path and takes a liberating vow of poverty, of political poverty. There is no distinctively Christian task of

mixing capitalist oil and socialist water. His is the freedom to choose the class with whom to cast his future.

This liberating suffering is not the end. There is still some dying to be done. The petty bourgeois is called the transition class. Although it has a distinctive role, it is limited and temporary. As contradictions heighten between capitalists and proletariat it is bound to die. Does it have no choice, then?

It can offer its life voluntarily. It can defect from the establishment it objectively served and "offer the capital it has stolen from the colonial schools and institutions to the revolutionary potential of the people" (Fanon), a la Victor Corpus. (Lt. Victor Corpus defected from the Armed Forces of the Philippines in December 1970 to join the New People's Army. This defection received much attention throughout the Philippines.)

But there is another, more literal meaning to dying: "It is essential that the revolutionary conviction of each student be so ingrained that he accept it in its totality, even to the ultimate consequences. Poverty and persecution must not be sought after. But, given the present situation, they are the logical consequences of a battle to the end against existing structures. Under the present system, they are the signs which given authenticity to a revolutionary life" (Camilo Torres).

The Christian is faced with an even more frightening death. His God dies. The God who revealed social principles and performed miracles of power is suddenly challenged by the power of people who try to make history. Mao's parable on *The Foolish Old Man Who Removed Two Mountains* poses the problem very explicitly. "Our God is none other than the masses. . . If they stand up and dig together with us why can't these two mountains be cleared away?"

The God of the fable he quoted, a God who sends angels to clear away the mountains of feudalism and imperialism,definitely has to die if people are to achieve liberation. Where does a God come in then? Through a Christ, whose greatest miracle is the miracle of loving unto death.

"He descended into hell." Chardin interprets this as Christ's touching the very depth of reality, the heart of the matter. Some activists say, "*Talagang sagad, kayod, yanig hanggang ugat ang pagka-Kristiyano ko.*" But with them, the paradox remains true: "One must be willing to lose one's life if one wishes to save it."

And what about resurrection? Where is the new petty bourgeois and the new Christianity? It's too early to say. Besides, the basic resurrection of a new people, of peasants and workers no longer passively accepting oppression but struggling for their dignity, is gathering momentum in many places.

And even now, there is a new people and a new consciousness. With power to take care of their own affairs, without need of the bread and relief goods and cooperatives of Christianity. A proud people that is self-reliant. To them, perhaps, the gospel of a crucified Christ can be preached without any reactionary or colonial overtones. The "powerless power" of the Gospel will be real in the face of the freedom of a liberated people. Is it that, or is it the final "withering away" as some activists predict?

In the meantime it is Lent and wandering through the desert, one sometimes looks back wistfully at the secure definitions one has left and remembers with some vacillation the theological, political and economic fleshpots of the Establishment. And grumbles at leaders and companions, and thinks of repentance and struggle, and hopes that the fight to level the hills and fill up the valleys will prepare the way for the coming Kingdom.

CHURCH AND LIBERATION IN THE PHILIPPINES
PPI National Convention, 1972

The original topic assigned to me was *Church: Liberation/ Development*, too broad for the limited time given. An overview of the development liberation question and the corresponding theology can be found in the two articles inside the convention kit: Gutierrez' "*Notes for a Theology of Liberation*" and Arevalo's "*Development, the Christian Vision.*" The Manifesto of 83 Theologians "*Against an Attitude of Resignation in the Church*" spells out better some details of the struggle for liberation within the institutional Church. This paper presupposes the insights of these three articles and invites you to discuss three theses:

1. The theological meaning of the terms *Church* and *Liberation* are very liberating and necessarily related to each other. But the actual operative meaning in Philippine society contradict each other. An exclusively theological use of the two terms objectively hinders the liberation process in the Philippines.

2. Liberation in present Philippine society calls for revolution.

3. The principal question for the institutional Church is not "What is the Church's role in Philippine liberation?" Most of the evidence shows that the institutional Church has been, is, and foreseeably will be basically opposed to the struggle for national and social liberation. What we need to define is the precise relationship between the struggle for liberation within the Church and the struggle for national and social liberation in our country.

Lumen Gentium and various theologians, especially "political theologians" and "theologians of hope" give us the following basic image of the Church: It is primarily a community of the people of God; it is a restless pilgrim and social critic because of its commitment to the Kingdom of God; it is not only critic but also bearer (sacrament) of the values of the Kingdom, a vanguard of the future that is already but not yet here; and it is essentially "for others" rather than "for itself."

Gutierrez and other Latin American theologians propose the concept of *Liberation* as the most promising synthesis of hitherto separate processes: the process of salvation and the process of development (humanization). Liberation expresses the unity of the human and the Christian vocation. The Church, then, is called to proclaim and effect man's total liberation.

One can get "high" reading and reflecting on the many articles on Church and liberation. But when the words become flesh and we look at their Philippine usage, we get opposite results.

"Church" *(ang simbahan)* means the institution (dioceses and parishes and religious orders and mandated organizations) and officials (cardinals and bishops and priests, brothers, seminarians, nuns, Catholic Action leaders) and physical plants usually of the Roman Catholic Church. It is not primarily (if at all) the millions who get baptized, married, and buried, the peasants, workers, professionals, squatters etc., — the Filipino people of God. It basically conserves the present system; instead of giving us a glimpse of the future, it generally reminds us of the past; and it is much more interested in preserving itself than serving liberation.

But when criticism arises ("what is the Church doing to solve national problems?"), the theological content is invoked: "The Church is not just the hierarchy; it is the whole people of God, or didn't you read Vatican II?" And yet this same theological truth is not recognized when peasants, workers and youth exercise in words and deeds the prophetic function of the Church.

The same problem plagues the term "Liberation" in the Philippines. Historically, it referred to the Filipino people's struggle against the Japanese occupation forces during World War II. The Americans however co-opted the term to make re-occupation acceptable to the Filipinos and to mask their neo-colonial presence. (It's most graphic symbol was July 4 as "Independence Day"). The *Hukbong Mapagpalaya ng Bayan* (HMB) also used *Liberation* for their struggle against American neocolonialism, against the landlords, and against the government. Liberation, then, was national and social (class); it was revolution.

There is a tendency, however, for the theological meaning of liberation to be understood as "human liberation" either in a very personalistic sense (from sin, selfishness, any restrictions to creativity) or in a very general a-historical sense. The precise anti-colonial, political and class content is lost in the dramatic vision of the total liberation of all men in Christ.

We are faced, then, with two problems: (1) The actual and historical meaning of liberation in the Philippines is opposed to the actual and historical content of the term Church, for the Church has been historically with the occupation forces and still is with the ruling classes. All the theological reconciliations and synthesis of Church and liberation will not change the objective antagonism between the Church and the movements for national and social liberation in the Philippines. If we insist on using the theological meaning of these terms we risk hindering the liberation process. How? By obscuring the contradictions ("the truth shall set you free") or by resolving the contradictions on paper and in mind, rather than in reality. An editorial in *Breakthrough* called for "an acted theology" and for the equivalent of a theological Marx to bring the theological Hegels down to earth. (2) The tremendous content of the theological meaning of liberation can prevent us from accepting and participating in the actual ambiguous process of liberation, the less than "total" programs and movements, the less than perfect struggles by less than perfect people for less than perfect goals.

What this all amounts to is the need to incarnate our theological concepts in Philippine society, so that our words really reveal rather than replace reality. In this way, we can avoid the accusation that our most beautiful words like justice and freedom and dignity are empty and powerless because they have no concrete historical and social settings.

Take, for example, the question of liberation and revolution in the Philippines. "Christian-moderate" activists shout: "*Sigaw ng Bayan:* KALAYAAN! (People's clamor: Freedom!) Radicals shout: "*Sigaw ng Bayan:* HIMAGSIKAN! " (People's clamor: Revolution!) And somehow the two slogans are considered contradictory. How do we achieve liberation? What is the aim of revolution?

To talk meaningfully of liberation in the Philippines is to start with an analysis of captivity and oppression. Here, the Church is often guilty of what we might call "romantic moralism." There are general denunciations of "social injustice," "oppression" and similar emotionally charged phrases but there is either shallow or simplistic analysis of the precise mechanisms of oppression and injustice. Hence, even the call for liberation is too general to be effective. And when it is specified by activists as national liberation from imperialism led by American monopoly capitalists, as social or class liberation of peasants and workers from feudal and capitalist modes of production and from exploitation by landlords and capitalists, the same people who called for liberation and issued declarations of concern and commitment turn against the specific movements and programs that would work out liberation in concrete. When the peasants and workers and youth shout that liberation is through revolution, the same preachers of the good news of liberation turn witchhunters and see red everywhere.

Perhaps with some reason. For we cannot deny that as of now, the systematic categories and historical outlook of Marxism-Leninism-Mao Tsetung Thought have been responsible for clarifying the problems and prospects of liberation in the Philippines. There is no need to summarize here Amado Guerrero's *Philippine Society and Revolution* which is right now the only systematic guide for further analysis of Philippine society. What we need to do is to overcome a triumphal search for totally different Christian categories and to submit ourselves to the same rigorous demands of analysis and concrete social and historical investigation which *Octogesimo Adveniens* acknowledges as the most attractive aspect of Marxism.

Without going through all the questions and insights that concern liberation and revolution in the Philippines, let me raise some key points for discussion. (1) The analysis of imperialism in the Philippines is essential to any serious talk of national liberation. We have to recognize that the Philippines is not simply an *un*-developed country that needs to be developed by capital and technology and direction from the developed country which then serves as model. Rather, the Philippines is *under*-developed; we are developing under the oppressive and exploitative weight of the developed countries so that with the rest of the Third World we

have to liberate ourselves from both means and models provided by the developed West. This means that nationalism is a basic factor in any liberation process for us and capitalism as a model system has to be rejected. (2) Political liberation cannot be separated from the class struggle since the national leadership that would struggle against the imperialist cannot restrict itself to "being in-charge" of the nation. It is supposed to construct a society along a socialist perspective. (3) There is no purely or even basically peaceful path to this goal of national liberation.

Does this mean that the categories of personal and human liberation (from sin and selfishness) have no place in national and social liberation? By no means. In fact, the cultural revolution that prepares for, intensifies and consolidates the political and economic revolution precisely calls for a basic struggle to be selfless and to promote the spirit of serving the people. But it is essential to realize that liberation revolution is a historical and social process. Freedom is not a state of total unrestricted enjoyment by everybody of all rights all at once. It is to be realized historically in the struggle between forces that bear the promise of wider liberation and forces that would restrict freedom to the few who are economically and politically powerful and therefore are free to prevent others from being free.

I wish I could be clearer about this point, because it is crucial for avoiding the futile waiting for a pure liberation process, program and movement. Real liberation and revolution is *simul justus et peccator*, because the process is dialectical. Some must decrease so that others must increase. If the developed are developed precisely because the underdeveloped are there to exploit, the liberation and real development of the underdeveloped can only be at the expense of the developed. Hence, the struggle for liberation and the precise nature of the conflict (degree of violence) cannot be determined only by the forces for liberation. But even though the decision for violence must be made while taking into account the expected reaction of the forces of oppression, the decision remains a decision. It cannot be simply a reaction that disavows responsibility as implied in the attitude "I'll exhaust all peaceful means until you force me to use violence." This leads either to exhaustion in futile reformism or leads to spontaneous, anarchic and often hopeless rebellion. But these are really questions that should be discussed in concrete historical and social settings. Otherwise we end up moralizing about violence and washing our hands like Pilate.

In the face of these unfinished reflections, what can one say about the Church?

There is no need to go into polemics here. We simply have to admit that the main bearers of liberation (especially national and social) in Philippine society are the peasants and workers and the different organized cultural and propaganda groups. We cannot locate the center of any liberation efforts in the institutions of the Roman Catholic Church in the Philippines. In fact, the Church is still basically a sacristan of the existing order.

Hence the need for a double repentance and what we might call a vow of political poverty: to turn back and say No to the existing power privileges. But there is also a very necessary renunciation of attempts to lead the liberation process or even formulate a distinct program. If we can repent, our role is to serve the basic forces for liberation: the peasants and the workers. This calls for a vow of obedience to their historical vocation to assume power and therefore disobedience on our part to a lot of "priorities" that serve as an excuse to avoid saying Yes to liberation.

Again, let me end with some points for discussion: (1) The Church institution must be analyzed scientifically and should be expected to carry the same contradictions as the society it serves. Hence the presence of neo-colonial, feudal and capitalist features in the Church. Hence the need for class analysis in the Church and among Churchmen. (2) The different struggles of seminarians, nuns, priests and lay people for due process, decision making, and other issues in the Church can succeed only if the forces for national and social liberation advance in their struggle in the society at large. (3) There is need for political and organized struggle within the Church if there is going to be more than paper liberation. Otherwise the priests, sisters, and seminarians who are committed to the struggle for national and social liberation in the Philippines should be prepared to either liberate themselves or be liberated from the institutional Church. I wish these were simply theoretical questions. But they are very present and very pressing personal struggles among those who, in one way or another, are both in the Church and in liberation.

Section Three

Companions in the Struggle

Laughter, hugging
in a storm
Hand on shoulder squeezing
Triggering tears.

Fingers on a guitar
Holding out a tune
Drowning in thunder

Fresh cut flowers
Nailed on a cross
A mountain of memories
A bonfire
burning in the wind.

LOOK UP TO THE HILLS. . . (Psalm 121)

I couldn't help exclaiming how small she was for a Filipino college student. She looked like a high-school kid, bright-eyed, with a round, brown face that any photographer would want for a pictorial on Central Luzon peasants. But she had a way of speaking, a quiet intensity, that made her seem older than many of the delegates at the SCM (Student Christian Movement) national congress in May, 1971.

She came up to me after my keynote address, to tell me she found my speech helpful. I had talked of Christians calling ourselves "servants of the revolution" (rather than servants of Christ or of the people), to emphasize that the service our times call for is participation in an ongoing process that we didn't start, but which we should continue. Besides, revolution is conveniently ambiguous. Theists could look at it and see God at work in history, breaking up the old and creating the new. Atheists or those with more secular worldviews could say it is people making history, the silenced majority breaking out of the culture of silence (Freire) to speak their word and name their world.

Later on, she and I would smile back at such, too mechanical, distinctions. But at that time, it was adequate for our concern to emphasize the primacy of the living, complex revolutionary process over rigid ideological definitions, to call for humble service that would not be servile, and to keep learning from those who had more experience, both the organized masses and the Marxists, reminding ourselves that we are latecomers.

We met a second time at the UP Tarlac, for a symposium. She came with a friend who waited shyly, then smiled when I recognized him. He had been to our seminary in Tagaytay, part of a group of Tarlac students a nun had hustled over for a retreat. She was concerned over their growing radicalism, and even more over their rejection of Christianity as it was presented to them. (They pictured it as worried old people who preach caution, "prudence," but refused to help them in their serious search for political commitment.) She hoped I could, perhaps, explain to them that choosing to be radical did not have to mean ceasing to be Christian?

He had interesting tales to tell — of getting delirious with fever in the midst of the rainy season, of being carried by carabao over slippery mountain trails, of his regret at having to leave the training camp. His stories were like sequences from an old movie, full of action and vivid detail, but coming across to me as less than real, because I had no personal experiences to relate them to.

"I'm quite recovered from my fever now," he said. "I should be going up again, soon." She added that she was considering doing the same, though a bit later. I thought with a sudden chill that I might not see them again. "Please call me before going up," I made them promise.

He called for me one late afternoon at Christ the King Seminary. "Let's go," he said as soon as I shook his hand. I quickly checked my schedule. "Sure. Where?" His answer stunned me. "To the hills."

I finally managed a weak, hoarse "Why? " He explained matter-of-factly that he had submitted seven names, mine among them, to friends up there. They recently sent word that they were ready to receive us. "I'm to escort you." He added with a half-smile that some peasants in the camps kept asking with disbelief if it was true that a priest was really joining the NPA, and would he be acting as chaplain, and would they have to build an altar for mass?

"But I'm not prepared to go." It was his turn to fall into puzzled silence. It took us a while to sort out our mutual confusion. It turned out that when I insisted on his calling me before going up, he thought I meant to join him. The prospect pleased him, and he passed on my name to his contact. Then came August 21, 1971 — Plaza Miranda was bombed, the writ of habeas corpus was suspended, the military were hunting 60-plus names on an arrest list, and even those who were not in it scampered for cover. He concluded that I'd have even more reason to go up.

I explained that I felt my place was in the open, legal movement, what we called then the cultural revolution. There were too few Christians (more precisely, church people) in the national democratic movement, and even they were branded as Communists. We needed to establish the legitimacy of Christian presence in the

radical movement, and challenge those who restrict Christianity to conservative and reformist politics. This is important for Christianity, but it is also important for the movement. We should not allow our enemies to brand the whole movement as Communist, or concede in disgust when they try to mobilize God, religion and the church against us.

It was not time for people like me to join the NPA. I know the NPA is not all Communist either, but few people make the fine distinctions. More important, the question of direct participation in armed struggle should not be made the immediate issue for Christians. It must be placed in context, after discussing the main themes of the cultural revolution — to expose and oppose the systems, the *isms*, that block national and social liberation, and to arouse, mobilize and organize the people into a united front for national liberation and democracy.

He didn't hold back his smile at my next point. "I'm not even physically prepared," I said. "I like ice-cold Coke too much!" Next time they think of inviting me, our friends should give me a few months warning, a withdrawal period from this addiction. We both smiled at the idea of slipping out of camp to buy Coke at some *sari-sari* store. (Later, in prison, I heard a kindred tale, of a college kid who joined the NPA, suffered battle shock, and begged for only one thing, a bottle of Pepsi.)

A few weeks later, I got another message, this time from her. She would be at a Protestant chapel in Caloocan that night. Would I see her? She wanted to say goodbye.

I quickly flagged a taxi to avoid the rush hour traffic. I wondered how she was feeling just before going up. How did her parents feel, did they give her decision their blessings? Her gesture of friendship touched me. I worried for her, but was even prouder. I thought of what to say, of the many things I wanted to say, finally discarding all as inadequate and unnecessary, simply wanting to see her again and hug her.

She talked in her usual quiet way, her voice a bit huskier, I thought. About how she was trained, and the hardest lesson — to be patient, to wait for hours on hours in some peasant's hut for

her guide. To walk steadily on rice paddies in the dark, keeping proper distance from the comrade ahead. To pick herself up without much fuss whenever she slipped and fell.

Her eyes were never brighter than that night as she talked of how the masses have been serving us for so long, her mind leading mine across centuries of Philippine history. Even now they feed us, give us use of their huts, guide us across the fields, warn us about enemy movements and hide us, tell us stories of past struggles, lessons summed up from many victories and setbacks, carefully stored in their patient memories. "It's now my turn to serve them," she said. In her gently spoken phrase, *serve the people* ceased to be a slogan appropriated from Mao and the Chinese revolution. It became Filipino, *utang na loob* (a cultural duty to reciprocate).

BECAUSE of her, I became part of those who would anxiously read the morning papers for news about the NPA. Always, there was tension at possibly reading her name or his name among those reported killed or captured, then relief that their names were not in the news, until next day's paper brought back the worry.

To defend ourselves against such constant worrying, we would reassure ourselves that guerillas know how to take care of themselves. Then the pace of the protest movement mercifully picked up to fill our days and nights with many other things to do and think about. To protest the suspension of the writ (a rehearsal for martial law, some called it), radicals and moderates met to form a coalition, the Movement of Concerned Citizens for Civil Liberties, with Senator Jose Diokno as head. It was good to see many familiar faces, some still friendly, among the moderates, even though I sat in an unaccustomed place on the other side, with the radicals.

One afternoon, I got a call to speak at a Plaza Miranda rally. I went to the underpass exit, in front of Quiapo church, toward Carriedo St., thinking that we'd be using its concrete roof (we usually did) as speakers' platform. But a wooden stage had been built on the other side of the plaza, and I had to snake my way through the thick crowd, the biggest I had ever been in yet. The

people looked more sunburnt and tired than the usual demonstrators. They had walked in a three-day long march all the way from Central and Southern Luzon.

As I climbed up the stage, I wondered if it was the same one the Liberal Party used that terrible night when grenades were thrown at them. Perhaps not, since the stage seemed too makeshift, though it stood on the same spot. Then I was on stage, caught up like the rest in the rituals of protest.

The speaker ahead of me was quite a surprise, a fellow priest, complete with white cassock, though quite dusty and sweat-streaked. He had marched with the Southern Luzon group, someone volunteered: he's principal of a high school in Batangas, a Benedictine. I made a mental note to ask Caloy Tayag if they knew each other. His speech was fiery, with a fervor fueled by the long march. One line set the crowd cheering extra loud. "If the AFP have their chaplains, there are those of us who are ready to be chaplains of the NPA!"

I clapped and cheered with the rest, then worried how to follow his act. There are no hard and fast rules about speeches at the rallies, but some ritualization nonetheless develops, and succeeding speakers are expected to raise even more "advanced" topics. First parts are usually given to denunciations, starting with concrete issues that get linked to systems — imperialism, feudalism, bureaucrat capitalism — all roundly condemned with resounding *Ibagsak!* With the suspension of the writ, fascism gets singled out, and some speakers drag in revisionism and clerico-fascism for good measure. Then comes the cheering, *Mabuhay!* for the alternatives, the solution: the Filipino people, the national united front, the people's democratic revolution, the people's war. If a speaker is daring enough, or gets carried away by the crowd's response, there are extra loud *Mabuhays!* for the NPA, a patently illegal organization. About the only name I hadn't heard so far in rallies was the Communist Party of the Philippines, although its chairman's nom-de-guerre, Amado Guerrero (beloved warrior) was being chanted more frequently, especially in student rallies, and the hammer and sickle often appeared with the graffiti.

The way the speaker was carrying on, he'd leave me nothing to add but the topic of leadership in the revolution. That meant the

CPP. I wasn't sure I could do that. The most radical slogan I had ever shouted publicly till then was *Mabuhay ang pambansang demokratikong rebolusyon!* I was quite prepared to ask. *Ano ang sagot sa martial law?* to set the crowd chanting *Digmaan, Digmaang Bayan!* I also knew that I could shout *Mabuhay ang NPA!* with genuine feeling, for I would be cheering for two dear friends, not just a faceless organization that I respected but didn't relate to emotionally till then.

But the CPP? That was something else. I didn't know any Communist personally. It would be half a year before I met someone who admitted he was a party member. Of course, like most activists, I presumed there would be CPP members in the legal mass organizations, not just in the NPA, and if only by default, the CPP had a rightful claim to being the party that led the revolutionary movement. But like most Christians, even radical Christians, I had too many emotional blocks to overcome despite being called a Communist or, at least, crypto-Communist by conservatives and most reformists.

As the speaker was winding up, I suddenly tuned out. I don't know what triggered it. I could still see the crowd, now intently listening, now cheering, clenched fists thrust into the air, chanting their *Amens* to the speaker's litany of slogans. But I didn't hear the sound and the fury except as a faint noise, as if someone had turned the volume knob of the TV close to zero. Even the red flags — there must have been hundreds — seemed to wave in slow motion against the darkening background, the sun having set and the saints' statues behind the crowd a blurred twilight grey now, except for the book one of them clutched in his stone hands; some activist had painted it red.

In that sudden silence, the thought crossed my mind. What if someone threw a grenade, as in the LP (Liberal Party) rally? I imagined the dark pineapple shape flung from where the statues stood, looking darker as it tumbled in a wobbly arc toward the stage where we sat transfixed until the fatal blast. My dead body would be counted with the radicals, I thought. But did I really count myself one of them?

In a rush, like a man whose life passes in quick review before dying, I went through a mental checklist of my political beliefs — analysis, strategy, tactics. No problem there. I understood and accepted the logic of the national democratic line. What about feelings, companionship? I had quite a few close friends now among the radicals, people I could face death with. But I had even more friends among the moderates, especially with the two organizations I had been chaplain to, the FFF and Khi Rho. That was the problem. Given the hostility and rivalry between moderates and radicals, I hesitated to identify too closely with the radicals, lest my moderate friends think I was cutting myself off from them. I felt I owed them enough time and patient explanation, so they could understand why I became a national democrat. I couldn't, wouldn't force a split by pressuring them into joining me right away or else be left behind.

The cheering and the clapping finally jolted me back to the rally. I congratulated the speaker as he handed me the microphone. I don't recall most of what I said that afternoon, except that at some point, without having planned to, I found myself telling the huge crowd about my friend, how she bade goodbye to me the night she went up to the hills. I remember noticing that the crowd was quite silent and didn't cheer as I thought they would. I said there were many ways to look at what she did, but as a Christian, I couldn't help thinking of another person who climbed another hill long ago, ready to offer his life so that others might live fully. Of course we should not think only of sacrifice and death, I added, though it is a judgment on our times and those who lord it over us, that those who dare to love and serve the people are hunted and killed. As Christians we believe in the resurrection, we have hope. As revolutionaries, we look forward to victory. One day, may that be soon, our friends in the hills will come down and we will rise to meet them, and celebrate our liberation. That must have been the first time I quoted Psalm 121: "Look up to the hills, from where salvation comes."

That drew quite a cheer. But it was another reaction that warmed me more. "Her parents were there," someone told me. "At the back of the crowd, near the statues. They had tears in their eyes when you talked about her." I felt I knew why. I had talked to other parents whose children became radicals. After a while, they

could live with that, even feel a quiet pride sometimes. But they harbored a nagging fear. No, not that their children might die or be arrested, although, of course, that would be painful. The deeper doubt, despite their love and respect for their children, was that they had become Communists. To their traditional Christian culture, that meant being atheists, fighting God and risking hell. Unfortunately, even the most socially-concerned presentation of Christianity did not help any. It stressed moderation and reforms as the Christian alternative to revolution which it condemned as Communist. The children themselves might not feel the need to interpret their commitment in Christian terms, and might even resent it as a sort of forced baptism, but their parents needed to reassure themselves that a revolutionary could still be Christian.

When the time came for the final slogans (they always reminded me of liturgical acclamations), it felt good to shout *Mabuhay ang Bagong Hukbong Bayan!* I hoped that some activists were taping the rally, and not just military agents, so that my friends in the hills could later hear me cheer for them. I took a deep breath before the last slogan: *Mabuhay ang Partido. . .*(and finally waffled) *ng mga Anak-Pawis!* Through the cheering, I told myself Bonifacio would have understood my choice of words.

After the handshakes and congratulations, I started down the stage, feeling slightly feverish and raw, like someone who has finally managed to say "I love you" face to face, or like an evangelical after publicly witnessing. The leaders of the rally would later tease their spokesman for being "tailist," allowing two priests to sound more radical than he did.

Halfway down the narrow stairs, I was met by a young activist, bright-eyed, with a fair wide-open face that I recognized from a weekend recollection some nun had arranged for Tondo students. He was a member of the KM chapter at Torres High Schol. "Your speech was OK." He shook my hands as I smiled thanks. "I thought you'd never graduate from reformism. Finally!" The mischief was obvious in his eyes as he plunged back into the crowd, and I felt my feet touch the ground.

A recent photograph of priests and nuns demonstrating in Manila (Reflex).

A MONUMENT FOR THE DEAD
A MOVEMENT FOR THE LIVING

Some Reflections on the Gomburza Centenary, 1972

THE MORNING of the Gomburza centenary, February 17, 1972, saw President and Mrs. Marcos unveil a monument to the three priest-martyrs at Plaza Roma in front of the Manila Cathedral. (Damian Soto of barbershop fame would later protest at the impropriety of both name and place). Early afternoon witnessed the march-rally of an emerging movement. Christians for National Liberation (CNL). Their battle cry. Alalahanin ang kabayanihan nina Gomburza at isulong ang pakikibaka tungo sa pambansang kalayaan at demokrasya! " (Remember the martyrdom of Gomburza and advance the national democratic struggle!) Manila Times later erroneously (felix culpa?) reported that PPI sponsored the rally.

THIS article is an attempt to pose the scattered questions about the monument and the movement. It is also an invitation to fellow priests and Filipino Christians for a continuing dialogue on the role of Christians and particularly churchmen in the struggle for national liberation in the Philippines.

Fr. Hilario Lim X.J. (Kumander Yayong of the cultural revolution) poignantly asked a lot of questions that afternoon. "Why don't they transfer your (Gomburza) bones to this monument and make it a cenotaph? Why do they hold symposiums on 'little known facts' about your life, but not about the implications of the great fact of your death? Why do they insist that all of your works are spurious? Is it because *La Loba Negra* talks of socialism? Why don't they publish your works?" The day before Ash Wednesday, (Feb. 16) additional questions were debated during the initial conference of CNL. How politically guilty were Gomburza? Was their protestation of innocence significant? Was their interest limited to Filipinization? to clerical nationalism?

Most of the questions remain unanswered. But the participants agreed that for all the lack of historically precise answers, especially about the relationship between church reform and political

reform for Gomburza, their death and martyrdom commits them irrevocably to the continuing movement (ever unfinished) for national liberation in the Philippines. Their death is so definite (so finished) that even those who would not look on them with favor were they still alive could offer flowers to their monument and attend masses and literary-musical programs and co-opt them into "revolutionary" speechifying.

The questions about the precise historical significance of Gomburza will continue to be asked. But the bigger and more important questions are about the present struggle of different Christian groups to discover and fulfill their historic role in the continuing movement for national liberation.

One such group is the CNL, Christians for National Liberation. It is still struggling for a more precise definition, but the questions that have been responsible for its birth are sufficiently clear. It has issued a "Gomburza Declaration" (February 17, 1972) signed by seventy-two participants in its initial assembly and is presently organizing units for study and praxis. In the spirit of another Christian who struggled for liberation, Dietrich Bonhoeffer, it has "taken the risk of saying things that are open to dispute, provided that vital problems are thereby raised."

What follows is the text of the declaration and a personal commentary:

> This declaration is a point of arrival and departure for us. It ends our separate search for authentic service to our people and starts our organized struggle along the narrow path to national liberation and democarcy.
>
> We recognize that we are not the first or the only Christians to struggle for national liberation and democracy. We only want to make public our organized commitment and offer this path to fellow Christians who want a more organized and disciplined participation in the struggle.

The first two paragraphs describe the search for a definition by the participants. Some pastors and priests have had contact with

the national democratic organizations (often accused as Maoists) and have agreed with much if not all of their political analysis. But this has led to some basic questions: How does a Christian relate to revolution? What about Christianity and Mao Tsetung Thought? Is Christianity antithetical to Marxism? And even if a Christian could decide to relate to the radicals, how would the radicals accept him? Is social democracy (with its inviting "Christian" color) not the better choice? Is Communism not the more actual enemy of the Christian not imperialism, feudalism and bureaucrat capitalism?

The organizational experience of two youth organizations of Christians focus the questions more sharply. The Student Christian Movement (SCM) or KKKP (Kilusang Kristiano ng Kabataang Pilipino) voted last May 1971 to join the Movement for a Democratic Philippines (MDP). For it, Christian commitment is incarnated in the national democratic struggle. This had led to rabid accusations that it is not Christian anymore but simply a Communist front, or, more charitably, a group of deluded Christians. Within its ranks, the questions also kept cropping up: Does our being Christian add to the movement any qualitative contribution?

Similar questions kept hounding the Kilusang Khi Rho ng Pilipinas (KKRP). It started out simply as a movement that sought to practice their Christian duty along the lines of the papal encyclicals. Then, both direct experience of Philippine reality and theological purification of their understanding of politics (there is no specifically Christian analysis, strategy and tactics, or model of a society) led to sympathy and openness to the radical groups. Again the accusations came from witch-hunters: You are infiltrated by Communists. You are too radical. From within, the questions also arose. How far can we read and use Mao? What does it really mean to be a Christian? To be a Church? What's worthwhile about liturgy?

Similar questions are being asked and will be asked from within and from without the other youth groups that are struggling to define CNL. The SCA, the Methodist Youth fellowship, the Christian Youth Fellowship, the IFI Kilusang Pambansa ng Kabataan, the Lutheran Youth Fellowship, different seminarian groups, especial-

ly those who were expelled or will be requested to leave because "they are too radical" — for them, the "narrow way" of Christian witness along national democratic lines will be filled with questions.

This declaration is being issued at the beginning of Lent and on the centenary of the Gomburza martyrdom in the spirit of criticism and self-criticism.

It is a declaration of repentance and self-criticism at being so slow and timid to respond openly to our people's call. It is also both commemoration and criticism of the Gomburza martyrs.

It would be a disservice to the heroic priest-martyrs and especially to our people if we only remember or repeat what they did and died for. Instead of protesting political innocence, we declare that radical renewal of Christianity and the churches cannot be separated from the struggle for liberation from imperialism, feudalism, and bureacucrat capitalism and from the political struggles of our people against their foreign and native masters. We declare that Christianity and our churches are economically and politically compromised by silence and direct consent to the present oppressive powers. We therefore explicitly commit ourselves to the oppressed classes' struggle for socio-political power.

In the same spirit of criticism and self-criticism, we renounce our triumphalist tendencies to consider ourselves as the main force or even the leading force in the struggle for national liberation and democracy. Although we recognize the necessity of daring witness in the spirit of Gomburza, we pledge ourselves mainly to serve the peasants and workers in fulfilling their historic role.

We recognize as our organizational task, our participation in the national democratic cultural revolution. But even as we define our organizational involvement, we acknowledge and support the actual and future efforts of fellow Christians who

commit themselves to direct political action in peasant and worker revolutionary struggle.

The conference began on Ash Wednesday and ended on Gomburza day. Lent for CNL will be a real "wandering and wondering"; it has left more secure and definite categories. Most of its members cannot claim definite commitment from their churches; they meet in the streets. But before they did march that afternoon, many of them had been wanting to express their protest and witness publicly to their convictions. However, questions and hesitations held them back. "*Anong sasabihin ng mga kaibigan ko? ng mga superiors?* " (Wht will my friends say? my superiors?) For priests, pastors and religious it was a question of "dignity," "impropriety." And since it involved radicals "We might be used." Alinsky had a graphic phrase for this: political virginity. We thought we loved. We thought we were concerned. But we would

not get publicly involved unless we were the ones in control of the situation. We were afraid of being violated, of being used. So we preserved our political virginity and loved secretly, from afar.

The criticism of Gomburza and the self-criticism are the result of a long confused period of struggle for self-definition. Were we primarily "Christians"? Or should we not be analyzed according to class, like the rest of men. Hence, petty bourgeois.

So long as we defined ourselves first as Christians, and asked first what the role of the Christian was, we were more than normally confused. There might be only one Christ, but there are all sorts of Christians. Landlord Christians and tenant Christians and middle-class Christians. Worker Christians and capitalist Christians. A Christian girl goes to the hills to join the NPA. Is "Christian" a univocal term? analogous? equivocal?

One possible result. Christian is concerned with Church; hence a separation of the tasks of Church reform and social reform. Hence a lot of rationalizations and "theologizations" of what are basically class hesitations of the petty bourgeois as Christian objections.

Accepting incarnation, and rejoining the human race, we subjected ourselves to class analysis and revealed our petty bourgeois origins, status or outlook. Hence the need for explicit decision for the oppressed. For we are not non-partisan, middle class. We are bourgeois, no matter how petty. Hence the renunciation of a leading role (a very Christian temptation). Workers and peasants are the main bearers of humanization and liberation. Hence our primary role in cultural revolution. This does not deny any personal decision or charisma for daring witness a la Camilo Torres or even effective leadership among peasants and workers. But that is for remoulded, "proletarianized" individuals. As long as we are in our class, we remain vacillating and hesitating. We need the steady partnership of the peasants and workers.

We recognize three main tasks in the cultural revolution.

1. To expose and oppose imperialism, feudalism, and bureaucrat capitalism.

We acknowledge our inadequate knowledge of a truly scientific analysis of our society. We must adopt and develop a scientific methodology of research and action to avoid piecemeal empiricism and romantic moralism in criticizing Philippine society. We also need to develop a more effective pedagogy of the oppressed.

2. To arouse, mobilize, and organize the masses for a protracted and disciplined struggle on all fronts. As an organization, we are composed of petty bourgeois Christians. To avoid vacillation and to strengthen our commitment to the very end, we must effectively link ourselves with the organized peasants and workers and with other organizations in the cultural revolution. We also have to discover newer and better forms of mobilization.

3. To constantly remould ourselves and others away from selfishness and pride to selflessness and humble service to the people.

We commit ourselves to revolutionary ecumenism, to criticism, and self-criticism with other organized groups. We must make special efforts to overcome neo-clericalism and Christian triumphalism in our relationship to the Muslims, other cultural minorities, and Marxists. Together with personal conversion, we will conduct social investigation into and struggle against institutional selfishness in our churches.

We issue this declaration with a deep sense of distrust in ourselves. We dare to commit ourselves because of our trust in the people who have revealed to us the Spirit's call to liberation.

CHRISTIANS FOR NATIONAL LIBERATION!

TO CALOY TAYAG — MISSING

I do not remember the precise day when word came that you were missing.* All I recall is that I held back my tears, trying to convince myself you might still be alive, despite the sinking feeling I could not control.

When I got out of prison, I said mass with your mother and family. Even then, I did not cry.

But now, memories and tears rush in a flood. I have been reading the papers from the CNL congress held in 1981. They mention you and Puri Pedro by name, martyrs of CNL, *unang alay* (first offering).

I'm sure you would have felt extra "high," had you been at that congress. I remember how excited and happy you were when we finally managed to hold CNL's first congress in August 1972. The participants looked exhausted after the debate on the draft program and constitution. But you still had the energy level to declare the congress a success and lead the closing cheers. You always had a sense of liturgy and ritual. It must have been your Benedictine background.

I remember marching with you in that procession to Plaza Miranda. We were very aware that it was the anniversary of that terrible night when grenades were thrown at the Plaza, but we were also determined to make our public pledge of commitment in that symbolic place. Who could have known then that just a month later, martial law would drive us from public witnessing into the catacombs of clandestine resistance?

When the first KKKP activists were killed in Mindoro, targets of the graduation exercises of a scout ranger team, you wrote a poem whose first line is the finest you've written. "Your deaths weigh heavy on us/Like a mountain." I think that line is your most successful fusion of Filipino, Christian and Maoist sensibility. It refers to Mao's imagery of death in the service of the people as significant, heavy as mountain, unlike the other kind of death that is

*Missing since 1976, allegedly abducted by military elements.

light as a feather. You managed to allude to that while speaking the truth that we feel more immediately when friends die, when our hearts ache under the heavy weight. Heavier still is not knowing if you are dead or alive. Not being able to go through the catharsis of crying over your body.

A third layer of meaning is Christian, although you and I never did find out who first translated Mao's mountain to Calvary, where Christ offered his life for the many, and "light as a feather" to "light as the rope Judas used to hang himself." Your poem was in my mind when I wrote about remembering friends, "And a thousand crosses/On a heaving mountain." Remember the nun from your home province of Pampanga who said that on the Central Plains, "The masses are our mountains."?

I dug up the commentary I wrote on the first CNL declaration on February 17, 1972. I wanted to use it as reference for a commentary I want to write on the 1981 program. The growth in insight and sharpness is obvious. You would have been pleased to read the decisive "political incarnation" of Christianity in the national democratic struggle. Also, your original ideas on church transformation are now systematized as "national democratic transformation of the churches," the special responsibility of CNL.

Friends usually smile when I tell them of your discussion on the "Protestant principle" and the "Catholic principle." How the Protestant principle allows us greater leeway for individual interpretation of our Christianity, making it easier for us to adopt a national democratic incarnation of it. On the other hand, the same liberalism prevents us from saying, as Catholics would: "This is the path, and no other." I know it was with you that I realized for the first time that we are Christians first, rather than Catholic or Protestant. The irony of it all was that we were helped in no small measure by the need to engage in our Philippine version of the Christian-Marxist dialogue.

Thinking of you, I also think of Puri, she with the laughing eyes. While we wrestled with the theology and politics of Christian participation in the revolution, she made us appreciate better the

companionship that made such struggle easier to go through. Do you remember your embarassed smile when she said the closeness she found in the movement was like what she looked forward to in marriage, minus the physical union? When news of her capture broke out, I thought we would have a reunion in prison, as soon as her bullet wound healed. But it never did. They made it bleed afresh, just before they strangled her.

Friends wrote about her funeral, asking about the resurrection. You and I talked about death more than once, when friends were reported buried in some distant mountain, some mutilated, others, still half-alive. We went through another dying as concepts and categories we were familiar with somehow did not seem so clear and secure. We understood John of the Cross' "dark night of the soul."

You used to say that what matters is that we go through that passage with companions. I told you about the last night of our picket at Agrifina, when the farmers and students gathered with torches for a final liturgy. They seemed so small, their circle of light barely pushing out the darkness. Why do we light those torches? Because we expect to drive away all the darkness? No, that would take many more people than we have. But our torches are bright enough to make us see that there are companions, bright enough for others far off to see that our group exists. It is not darkness that is most fearsome. It is the thought of being alone in the dark. Who knows how many might decide to join, because they need not face the harder prospect of starting from the scratch? As you said when we were thinking of new legal organizational forms for CNL under martial law, founders usually need to be saints. It's easier for us to join something that has gotten off the ground.

It's still a long journey, although we travel now with many more companions. You also have company. Our list of martyrs grow. I hear your voices in our prison song. *Huwag kang lumuha/Nasa inyong tabi/Kasama't kaakbay sa madilim na landas/Tungo sa maningning na bukas.* (Weep not/For we walk with you/Our comrades in the dark/Someday, we shall see the dawn.)

they have not
silenced
a just man

just because
they have
killed him

THE GIFT OF FINAL PERSEVERANCE

NILO VALERIO is dead. Those who killed him desecrated his body. They cut off his head. They have even stolen his body, leaving an empty grave.

How I wish that such an empty grave would be like another empty tomb one Easter Sunday, a sign that Nilo has risen again and is in our midst. But we still have to look for his body so we may give him proper burial.

Those of us who believe and hope in the resurrection, have something to hold on to while grieving over his untimely death. Many will say that it's a pity someone so young and so dedicated should die so suddenly.

I feel I know Nilo quite well, even though we have not been in touch since his seminary days. Even then, he was already firm and clearsighted about the path of commitment he would take.

For those of us who seek to tread that narrow path to liberation, Nilo is an example of what we have to strive and pray for — the gift of final perseverance.

He started on his journey ahead of most of us. I'm sure that he had his share of frustrations, difficulties, doubts and vacillation. The struggle is protracted, full of twists and turns. We travel with fellow humans who are undergoing transformation while seeking to transform society. More than once, we will be tempted to give up, drop out, hold back.

We need the gift of final perseverance.

His death reminds me of questions we used to ask before martial law, when talk of armed struggle and the risk of dying was still just that — talk — even among committed church people. We asked each other about Christ's death, and why we speak of his death on the cross as overcoming death.

One of our answers then might be worth recounting as we celebrate Nilo's total gift of himself.

If we look at our life as some precious treasure we must hoard, the demands made by others of our life are like losses. And death is a final loss, final failure to hold on to our life.

But if we look at our life as a treasure we must share, every service we give to others is a fulfillment of our life's purpose. And death is the final giving, the total giving. *Consummatum est.*

Nilo died fighting for the people he had committed himself to serve, the least of our brothers and sisters. To him and his loved ones, we speak Christ's words: *Those who hold on to their life will lose it; those who risk their life in the service of the people, will find it.*

Nilo hindi ka malilimot,
Kasama ka
hanggang sa dulo ng landas
*Hanggang sa tagumpay.**

*[Nilo, you will not be forgotten.
You are with us
to the end of the road
— until we reach victory.]

PRAYER FOR OUR TIMES
Philippines 1984

We raise our eyes in prayer
through the bars, darkly

Together with a thousand prisoners in their cells
and with many more thousands in the larger prison
of our country.

We pray for freedom
and even more urgently, for life

As nameless executioners salvage
those whom they used to merely torture and detain
and both children and parents
slowly but surely die
of sickness that has many names
and only one name.

We ask for faith
to see that death and prison are not forever
that life and freedom will prevail

We ask for faith
tc celebrate even while we mourn
knowing that death and prison
are already signs of a people's struggle
for freedom and life.

We raise our voices in prayer
through the bars, boldly
believing that there will be an answer
as our people awaken.

Amen.

Section Four

through the bars, darkly

There are smaller prisons
for those who would break down
bigger and thicker walls
not to escape
from the rest
but to open up the world
and its future
to people whose hopes
have faltered in the dark.
Walls break down
when people's hopes rise with the dawn
melting falsehood and tyranny
with angry noon-heat
of caring.
There are smaller prisons
and tighter bars
to keep the spark
of those who dare love
from lighting a devouring flame
that consumes rust
and purifies gold.

TO HUNGER AND THIRST FOR JUSTICE

Letters and Poems from Camp Olivas, Pampanga

On Torture: "I rejoice. . . that my body is made to bear marks that will identify me more fully with the oppressed."

Mga Kapatid sa pananampalataya,
*Mga kapatid sa pakikibaka,**

I write, first of all to the different religious houses and Church people with whom I have dialogued these past 2 1/2 years.

The military might harass you on the excuse that I have squealed information (as they are trying to make me do) on my friends.

Tell everyone I haven't given any name, place or event as of now. I cannot absolutely guarantee my steadfastness under more forcible measures, but rest assured that I am preparing myself spiritually for torture and even death.

The dictatorship's forces have arrested me. Up to now they are trying to extract information from me and from other prisoners so they can fulfill the "legal" requirements to convict me.

They assure me that they will follow the Church-Military agreement (which they have already violated during my arrest) and will treat me courteously.

I haven't been tortured till now. Other prisoners arrested in this last series of raids (around 22 in all) are not so lucky. At least one of them, Reynaldo Ilao, a worker, got a "massage" that left him with bloodied eyes, cut brows and a possible broken rib. A second older man has a bandaged swollen foot. A third walks with noticeable limp. I don't think these are natural disabilities.

*Brothers and Sisters in faith
Brothers and Sisters in the struggle

A little bit of what might be happening reached me on the night of the 14th. I was half-asleep in bed when an interrogator came in and asked me two questions. I answered a bit sleepily. He punched me in the stomach. I screamed, "My God! " and doubled over in pain. He followed with a blow to the back of my head. My scream drew attention. My assailant told the others. "The father has ulcers." He left with a parting jeer. "Why does he call on God? I thought he was a Party member."

The pattern is becoming clear. Officially and to the best of their ability, they will treat churchmen well. But "communists, radicals, subversives, etc." — they are not supposed to have rights. If priests are beaten, well, it's because he is a radical.

I think the church should refuse to be party to this hypocrisy and discrimination. If we believe that torture is wrong (and even Marcos denies that it happens), then it is wrong not just on church people but on all. Otherwise we fall into the trap of the dictatorship that classifies people into Yes men and "subversives," and denies all basic freedom to those it suspects.

In the different interviews I have had (ranging from 5 minutes to 8 or more hours) — I tried to explain without much success I fear, the reasons for my involvement. Most of them, however are not interested in reasons, they want betrayal of information on friends, contacts, allies.

I told them what I have tried to live for and what I hope I am ready to die for, not just a genuinely free and democratic Philippines, but also an authentically radical Christianity.

I said that Christianity — both institutionally and theologically — has hitherto been either outrightly with the established oppressors or has contented itself with a middle-of-the-road position. What a growing minority is searching for, however, is a position that is radically committed to liberation both as an expression of and as a path to radical Christianity.

There are risks in this "pilgrimage." There are consequences, including torture and death in the hands of those who would make

Christianity a justification for state violence against "communist, subversives, atheist, etc."

I think, however, that in situations of injustice and oppression (which even my interrogators admit still exist), the path to justice and freedom is not easy or, pleasant.

I rejoice, in fact, that my body is made to bear marks that will identify me more fully with the oppressed.The word can become more literally flesh and blood.

Sometimes, fear sweeps over me. I recall Rev. Cesar Taguba who was transferred from camp to camp and passed Olivas, too. He was forced to drink his own urine, was given truth serum and underwent other hardships. I remember Ronnie Hilao, Liliosa Hilao's brother, who was bloodied and beaten up here before he was brought for further "treatment" to 5th CSU, Crame. In snatches of communication with other prisoners, I gathered that at least 2 of them got electric shocks on their genitals. In fact, when one of them saw the wounds healing on my wrists (from hand-cuffs), his spontaneous question was — "Electric wires? "

I got even more worried when Col. Aure of 5th CSU told me they were going to take me. I know of at least 2 cases of 5th CSU-NISA torture. And after 5th CSU-NISA, ISAFP will want to have their turn. Up to now Ric Dantes bears in his body and literally in his heart the effects of their efficiency.

But somehow the fear leaves me when I think of the many more who have remained steadfast under suffering and even unto death. Even death become a chance to find out the answer to a very personal, theologico-ideological question of what resurrection really is.

I don't want to be morbid, however. I don't think the dictatorship is ready to torture me or kill me yet, at least not officially. If it happens, it will be blamed on personal over-zealousnes or excused as a mistake. "But, I assure you it will never happen."

Or perhaps they will say: "He's too unreasonable." But I ask you: Is it unreasonable to refuse to betray friends and allies? Is it un-

reasonable to give them information they will use to stab me with?

If they have evidence, and they claim to have more than enough, then let them dispense with the hypocrisy and charge me,convict me, and punish me.

All I ask, and this is the final reason for this letter, is that I be allowed to speak (without benefit of interpreters, mediators, etc.) to people who are very real to me, so that I can attempt, even if I falter, to turn over to them the questions or initial answers of our continuing passionate search for justice, truth and freedom.

In the struggle,

FR. ED
Z-2
Camp Olivas
December 18, 1974

P.S. I do not know when precisely it will start, but sometime after this I will go on a hunger strike to protest the torture and indefinite detention of political prisoners.

Celebrating the Eucharist in Prison: "Despite the caution that I shouldn't give a sermon (being a detainee), I had to express my anguish at celebrating a sacrament of brotherhood and unity in the midst of conflict — between captors and captives."

Dear Archbishop Sin,

A Blessed Christmas!

I have just come from midnight mass. The authorities at Camp Olivas allowed Fr. Lahoz and myself to celebrate the Eucharist with the detainees of the Intelligence Division and with some enlisted men and their families.

I'm still quite tense and raw over the experience. Despite the caution that I shouldn't give a sermon (being a detainee), I had to express my anguish at celebrating a sacrament of brotherhood and unity in the midst of conflict — between captors and captives. I told them that Christmas should make us face up to the reality — flesh and blood, our concrete situation.

I told them I didn't want to further heighten the conflict and tension, but neither did I want to use the liturgy as a mask to prevent us from seeing the truth.

Anyway, we made it through with some goodwill to spare, and the 30 or more recent prisoners who have hitherto been incommunicado had a short reunion after mass.

In the midst of the greetings, some jarring notes refuse to escape notice — our guitarist's shoulder was black and blue (from beating, I presume). One or two people complained of what felt like broken ribs. Another was limping on a bandaged foot which was burned with a flat iron.

I have read your stand against torture. Please try to bring these cases to justice.

I do not want to spoil your Christmas joy by bringing up these ugly realities. I only offer them as a help to the ongoing incarnation of our reflections.

There is another reason for this letter, and I feel it too urgent to wait till morning. Some of my visitors told me that you once said, "This Fr. de la Torre never came to me while he was underground, but now that he is caught, he runs to me for help." I was told that you also called me a "Maoist."

I presume that you have been hearing a lot about me, especially from the military (who, I hear, are preparing a systematic smear campaign against me). So I feel the need to write to you as a Church leader, so that I can make up for the lack of communication.

I'm sorry for not coming to you this past year. I never even thought of doing so since I presumed you wouldn't jeopardize your legal status by meeting with hunted people. Besides, with the increasingly forthright stand you were taking against torture and distortion of news, I was conscious of the intelligence agencies' efforts to find "mistakes" in your behavior.

I'll be grateful for any help you would give but please do not feel obliged. I understand the ticklish position you have been thrust into.

I feel a greater need to share with you what I have tried to make my interrogators understand — that my involvement in the underground (which I do not deny) is deeply rooted in a serious effort to wrestle with this question: "How should Christians live in a situation of injustice and oppression? "

Know that the military is concentrating on proof: that I am in the underground, a subversive, linked up with the communists (one even claimed I was a candidate member of the central committee of the CPP) I'm sure they will have enough witnesses (tortured or not) and evidences to triumphantly convict me.

But that is not the point at issue. I have tried to make them understand that this is not a simple black and white question — am I subversive or not? Do I associate with the communists or not?

I told them that my involvement, like that of many Church people, started with reformist organizations. We read the Papal encyclicals, reflected on the gospel and advocated the need for people's organizations in order to achieve social justice.

But the various frustrations and even actual violence that met such efforts at reforms made some of us consider a more radical alternative. It was a choice full of risks and questions. Our very theology of liberation was just in birth pangs.

Then came martial law. At first, I didn't think of going underground. In fact, I went to Christ the King Seminary that morning (Sept. 23). The seminarians warned me that the Metrocom had come to arrest me.

I decided to hide, but not just to escape arrest. The bigger value was to pursue the task that remains ever valid — the development of genuine organizations of the people that will enable them to participate democratically in shaping a just and free Philippines.

In this process, I had a second concern — to establish links among different groups in the underground, to arrive at points of unity while identifying differences. I worked for the establishment of a united front of different dedicated groups and individuals: Christians, Muslims, Marxists and Nationalists — all Filipinos willing to risk their lives so that others may face the future with hope.

I know this letter has tried to say so many things too hurriedly. But I feel I must reach you before too many "interpreters" intervene.

Grant me (and my companions) this much — that we have tried as honestly as we could to confront the challenge of the gospel and the challenge of our people.

We offer our words and our lives as a small contribution to our common effort to make Christ incarnate in the Philippines.

In the Incarnate Word,

(Sgd.) FR. ED DE LA TORRE
Z – 2
Camp Olivas, San Fernando
Pampanga

December 25, 1974

P.S.1 I am starting an indefinite fast to bring attention to the torture and indefinite detention of political prisoners. Please help especially those who do not have relatives to follow-up their case.

P.S.2 And keep cracking jokes, they sound OK even when third-hand! Perhaps I'll hear some directly from you sooner or later (better sooner).

Copy furnished: SVD
AMRSP

To Hunger And Thirst For Justice

I have never been this hungry before
pain burning my guts, searing my back.

Food is doubly delicious
tuyo or crispy pata
corn soup and sinigang
turo-turo meals and banquets.

To starve after justice
to ache for it, like food, frantic for life itself.

How long can men live without eating
two weeks or more, they say.
But would such be living?
Too weak to rise from sleep
to read Bible and newspaper
to write with real meaning and beauty
to share and master the earth
to sing in the sun?

How long can men live without justice?
Can we ask them to wait again
while we ponderously weigh issues
which are complex, we say, and take time
which cannot be rushed
because we fear to be one-sided
etcetera?

Blessed are those who hunger and thirst after justice
for they shall be satisfied.

But when, O Lord, and how?

"THEOLOGY IS LIKE POETRY"
Letter from Camp Bagong Diwa, Bicutan

Dear Ely,

Walls and barbed wire are rather easy take-off points for writing on captivity and liberation, themselves quite familiar themes of our times and theology. I guess it is reasonable to expect three years and 10 months of prison life to yield some reflections. Except, I'm not sure they can be / should be "theological."

Some bible texts do come alive when read behind bars. The Messiah's mission in Luke 4,18 announcing freedom to captives reminds us of the many times we anxiously scanned release lists for names that were not there, or strained to hear radio announcements that never came. Churchpeople who visit are an occasion for a reverse perception of Matthew 25 — we've gotten used to thinking of visiting prisoners as a saving act, but not quite of being in prison ourselves! Still, this type of theologizing doesn't seem adequate or necessary.

I remember struggling over this question with Caloy Tayag — the contradiction between the need to deal with life in direct, descriptive and analytic, terms (scientifically, a Marxist would say) and the indirect, evocative language of what we usually call theology. Another poet-activist friend's insight into poetry proved helpful — There are times, she said, that are so

pregnant with meaning and feeling that bare reportage results in a poem. There are also times that need to be related to other symbols and images to reveal their poetry.

Perhaps that is enough for our purposes. To reflect on prison and the struggle for freedom in their own terms, their own reason and passion. Then, to relate these to symbols and texts that a particular people (a church) collectively remembers.

PRISON separates us from one community and introduces us to another — not just fellow political prisoners, but also those we call non-political, or lawless or criminal.

Martial law regimes try to deny the distinction, claiming that there are no political prisoners, only criminals. Sure enough, subversion, sedition and rebellion are listed as crimes in the penal code along with theft, robbery and homicide. Our reaction is to protest: "We are not criminals!" We point out differences, starting with very visible ones. Most criminals are tattooed, except those called *cuerna*. (Some soldiers respond that we too have tattoos, only we carry them on our brains!) And there are deeper differences.

But there are insights to be gained in reflecting on our unity with criminal prisoners before emphasizing distinctions. I don't mean the romantic notion of all men in chains being brothers, or some similar quotation. What we have in common is to have broken the law, or at least disregarded it.

For most Christians, breaking the "law" is associated with sin. Paul's pretty harsh remarks on the law tend to be interpreted narrowly, restricted to Jewish law. I have experienced this attitude not just within myself but among friends who, for all their sympathy, place great value in proving that I haven't really broken the law.

Of course we do give battle to our prosecutors on every legal point, knowing that most if not all of their evidence is illegally taken. But granting that we have broken the law, what does that mean?

What is the law, anyway, which we are supposed to have broken? Or the court which will provide formal excuse to detain us? What is this prison whose walls mark the boundaries of our lives? Or the soldiers and police who arrest, torture and guard us?

They are all but parts of one apparatus — the state, charged with maintaining peace and order, with upholding the law. But there is growing insight even among churches that only too often, the state seeks to maintain an existing disorder, a system that exploits and oppresses people.

This isn't a casual connection, for the origin and existence of the state is tied up with the rise of classes and class struggle, and classes point to the existence of exploitation. This is quite obvious in a semi-colonial and semi-feudal country like the Philippines. The implications for a society that is building socialism (and classes do exist during that process) would need another time.

This link between the law (the state) and the system it protects provides the bond between political and criminal prisoners. In our struggle to oppose and change the system, political dissenters are accused of crime, of breaking laws. In the breaking of laws by "common criminals," we see political dissent, in a spontaneous and distorted form.

It would do us much good to draw some parallels between this corrective insight and the as yet unachieved "balancing" between personal sin and "sin of the world" in our theology. To live in class societies and to be "law-abiding", as against the poet's cry: "Against the tyrant (and the system he maintains), to rebel is holiness!"

THE label "political prisoners" describes a variety of people. There are those we can best call victims — people who don't

have clear political convictions, but who have been sucked into prison anyway by the indiscriminately expanding military machine. There are those who criticize some aspects of the system or the whole of it, but haven't decided on definite alternatives. Others not only have chosen alternatives, but have struggled to gain political power in order to succeed.

There are church people whose attitude toward political prisoners reminds me of the traditional Feast of the Holy Innocents. They pour out their sympathies and indignation when the victim of illegal arrest, torture and indefinite detention is "innocent" of political views. Or, if he has political beliefs, he should not have acted on them against the law. Not UG, they say, not underground. I tease them on this, pointing out that Christ had "connections" and was warned in time. He "sidestepped," but the innocents got massacred. They usually are.

But seriously, we need to struggle against this one-sided celebration of innocence. And not just the pure, naive kind. What is more widespread among church people is the belief that while we should be critical of some aspects or even of the whole of a system, we should draw back from choosing alternatives and even more from struggling effectively to realize them. Somehow, this is considered a loss of "innocence," of what we may call political virginity.

But can we really dissociate ourselves from definite choices? Avoid sharing the "guilt" of any choice? Is there a pure, innocent position that can criticize all sytems from a supra-historical, unincarnate sphere?

This is where "theology" often reinforces our illusions. Instead of "being like the rest of men," accepting historical and social definition, we deceive ourselves and get scandalized all over at incarnation.

This a-historical thinking leads us to talk of absolutes — captivity or liberation, to be imprisoned or to be free. The truth is that being captive and being free are two aspects of a single process.

When some Tondo foreshoreland leaders and *batilyo* activists got released, we celebrated their freedom. A week after, one of the women-leaders visited us. She ruefully described the second adjustment her stomach had to make. Before she got detained, she had gotten used to drinking coffee (or hot water) to calm her stomach, because she could eat rice only once a day. There was not enough for three meals for her children. Inside prison, even with only four pesos government budget, there was too much rice for her and she had stomach pains for weeks as her body adjusted. Now she had similar pains as her body missed the three feedings. There are more such stories that justify one activist-prisoner's outburst. "We are all prisoners, only some prisons are smaller." Not to talk of being under martial law.

And yet we are also free, yes, even in prison. I don't want to yield to the usual platitudes about our spirit being free, or a fellow prisoner-poet's insight that our guards are more prisoners than us. No, we must not separate freedom from its material conditions. The same slumdwellers and factory workers who gripe about how "imprisoned" they are outside always end their litany of complaint with a shared truth. "It is better to be out of prison than in. Even if our cells shelter us better from the typhoon and even if our food improves!"

Where does our freedom essentially lie? In our decision to struggle as a community, for our own immediate welfare, for our release from prison. For our attempts to maintain our links with the people's struggles outside these walls that seek to separate us from them. That seek to "rehabilitate" us into being "practical" and thinking of ourselves, and withdrawing into the narrow cell of our personal interests.

I think I have to end here because there is too much to say. Anyway, the other prisoners' letters and poems will take care of what's unsaid. Looking over what I have written, I realize that I still wound up without much "theology." Perhaps this is just a reaction to too much God-talk that doesn't speak to our life, here and now.

Last week, our new ordination class asked me to share some thoughts on priesthood. A quick review of my life made me realize

that four years of my ten year-old priesthood has been spent in prison! I thought for a while, there must be some theology in that! Anyway, I like to end this with something I wrote them: There are no perfectly identical paths, and I do not claim that service to the people and incarnation in their struggle necessarily leads to prison. But it did lead me to captivity. Is it foolish to believe and hope, that the same service and the same incarnation point the way to our liberation?

"PRISON IS A WOMB"
Prose and Poems from Bago Bantay

NEW YEAR 1983

LAST night, after midnight mass, we were allowed to stay out of our cells for a while. We crowded around the top of the stairway, straining to see the fireworks through the prison windows.

After some efforts at gaiety, we all felt silent and yielded to what we really felt.

Alone in my cell, I thought of a poem I once read by Clarita Roja. She says the victory of the people's struggle will be like New Year's eve in Manila.

I could relate to that image — people celebrating in the streets, happy and noisy, even with the sounds of sporadic fighting. One can easily be caught up by the spirit of the crowd, if one is in their midst, part of them.

But from afar, the same happy sounds have a different effect — a certain sadness, at being left out or merely watching. Even if we were not imprisoned, we would feel that way.

A fellow detainee observed that the sounds and colors reminded him of Mindanao during the pitched battles between the MNLF and the government troops. People were frightened, even far from the battle sites.

I wondered if that would be true also of the people's victory. Will only those who take part feel the celebration? Will bystanders or those who opted to keep their distance feel sad? or scared?

APRIL 1983

AT ten p.m. the guard tells us to enter our cells. The bolts squeak as they are pushed into the concrete wall. The bunch of keys strike against the bars on the doors as the guard locks us in. The metallic sounds always jar. More often than not, I and my co-detainees frown at lock-in time.

Around seven a.m. the late-risers among us (most of us) are awakened by the same squeaky bolts being pulled out of the wall. The same bunch of keys strike against the bars as the same guard opens our doors. I am reminded of tiny bells or the ice-cream vendor.

Someday I should write a poem about that.

JULY 1984

A year ago, a nun-friend gave me a T-shirt for my birthday. The printed message was inevitable — "Life begins at 40." Looking back, I have to agree. 1983 saw new life. Not really for me, but for the legal popular movement that I identify with.

Who could have anticipated that outburst of popular protest after August 21? Friends who lived through the First Quarter Storm (1970) sounded like enthused critics comparing two similar movies.

Before Ninoy Aquino was shot, I thought the movement that would take off was MAPCO (Movement for the Abolition of the Presidential Commitment Order). MAPCO became the core of JAJA (Justice for Aquino, Justice for All), which in turn was the organized center of what came to be called the "new legal opposition."

Death and resurrection, an appropriate paradigm. Two deaths, in fact, and two resurrections.

The most obvious was the new life given the traditional legal opposition. Ninoy could not have done for them, were he alive, what his death did. Alive, with the same message of reconciliation, he would have been suspected of striking secret deals with Marcos. As a presidential aspirant, he would have his rivals. In death, his image was fixed as a symbol of opposition, and all opposition leaders invoke his blessings.

I was happier over the new life experienced by the new legal opposition. They also rose following another death, one earlier

than Ninoy's, September 1972, when martial law killed formal democracy. Many took the logical and dangerous step of building a clandestine resistance network. But we all agreed that an open, legal movement was necessary. More than ten years went into building one. Mistakes were made. Friends were arrested, tortured, disappeared. One couldn't really say which was more risky, clandestine or open work.

Suddenly, a flow. Friends who had been used to small groups and indoor gatherings could be forgiven for feeling somewhat dizzy in the midst of thousands marching on the streets.

Political prisoners also allowed themselves to hope anew. All protest movements were asking, "Free all political prisoners!" Prison can be a womb. But not for too many years. Hope can die, like a long-overdue child.

SEPTEMBER 1984

LAST week was Boy Morales' birthday, same day as Marcos'. Friends who came to celebrate sought to find some hidden meaning in that, like the prophecy in Macbeth.

At mass, I tried to speak to his relatives who are born-again Christians. Using John 3, "unless a man is born again," I said maybe that's one way they could understand what Boy has gone through. Leaving one life to pass through a second birthing, not quite finished yet. Marxists call it class transformation, from bourgeois to proletarian. Except, unlike our first birth, the second involves choice. Not just one act, but many, like renewing vows.

THROUGH THE BARS, DARKLY

Through the bars, darkly
I remember friends
and a thousand crosses
on a heaving mountain —
a gentle people
raging into the night.

The bars are dark stripes
and stars pierce the night sky
like wounds
on a giant bird of prey.

The bars are cold as nails
cold as gun barrels
on dismembered bodies
of missing friends
I struggle to accept
why the dead must bury the dead
why hope must dig furrows, not graves
and sow seeds to their cycle
of death and uprising.

Through the bars
the morning light slices
the stone walls like bread
I notice the crust of whitewash
crumbling.

OF BIRDS AND BARS

IT was Ed Maranan who first used this title for his collection of prison poems. That's about the most succinct definition of a prisoner's world. Bars for captivity. Freedom, a bird.

Birds are a universal symbol. But I think our bird-image had a more immediate source — the lyrics of Jose Corazon de Jesus for *Bayan Ko. Ibon mang may layang lumipad, Kulungin mo at pumipiglas* (Cage a bird that's free to fly and it shall struggle). The bird in that *kundiman* has become so associated with freedom from detention and dictatorship that its original nationalist intent is somewhat overlooked.

The original lyrics had the bird crying, *umiiyak* (crying). It was pre-martial law activism that questioned that. How will the bird ever get out if it merely cries in its cage? It must struggle to be free. Hence, *pumipiglas* (struggling).

The emphasis on militancy (Dare to struggle) was a necessary corrective to our culture of sadness. But a one-sided stress can backfire. Some *Gintong Silahis* singers were asked to perform at a Tondo fiesta. When the emcee introduced them, some people in the audience whispered. "*Ayan na ang mga nakakatakot*" (Here come the scary ones). We can't wallow in our grief, but we can't skip that either. There is time for crying. Otherwise, what grief shall we turn into revolutionary fervor?

Bicutan had two songs that consciously developed *Bayan Ko's* imagery. One was *Ibong Malaya*. Since Bicutan was supposed to be a showcase, its lyrics insisted *Ginto man ang hawla / Laya rin ang hanap / Bagwis ma'y malagas / Pilit na Lilikas* (Though the cage be golden / It shall seek freedom / Even if its wings are torn / It shall struggle to escape).

The other song had no title. It was composed by an NPA in Cagayan Valley, supposedly while undergoing his basic party course. A tape of his songs got to us in prison. When we were learning this song, we felt that the lyrics needed some changes. The original had the captive bird fighting to get out only because

it was being transferred to another cage. We thought that wasn't how prisoners feel.

It was Pepe Luneta who came up with the new lines. I remember that we tested alternative lyrics on each other while we were frying *galunggong* for lunch. The final version was *Kaya't ang ibo'y nagpasiya / Loob niya'y inihanda / Siya ay nanlaban / Hanggang makawala* (The bird decided / Strengthened itself / Struggled / Till it became free).

Those lines about decisions and "ideological preparation" came from way deep down. Prisoners like Pepe who could not realistically hope for legal release were under pressure to escape. Yet, they were the ones usually guarded tightly. After some years inside, other prisoners start questioning their determination to escape.

He once wrote a simple poem, *Burong Biya.* One prisoner who later escaped told us that the *biya* is a fish that is so stupid it dare not leap over a simple string stretched before it. Pepe's poem had him recalling that prisoner's story while he ate *burong biya* (fermented fish), still unable to cross the bars. It took him a few more years, but he made the jump.

Dante and the Dam

Ibong Malaya had a second image of freedom — water, a river rushing to the sea. When we were revising the lyrics, someone recalled **Kumander Dante's** interview. He said martial law is like a dam, set up to stem the movement.

Kung ang daloy ng tubig / Pilit na sagkaan / Taasan man ang harang / Hahanap ng daan / Tubig na naipo'y Higit na lalakas / Tibayan man ang harang / Sa huli'y sasambulat (If the flow is dammed / It will find a way through / The water shall gather strength / No matter how strong the barrier / It shall shatter).

I like those lyrics. The first reaction to the dam is very Filipino, *palusot.* I am told that when peasant associations are not yet strong enough, or are not ready to confront landlords to demand

their fair share of the harvest, the NPA advise them to employ *palusot* (a clever way through) — harvest their share secretly. But eventually, they build enough courage, and also organization to make the landlord yield.

Palusot is the initial way to resist. But it can't go on forever. Even if many can make *palusot*, that will not remove the dam. The only way the dam will burst is when enough water builds up to break it. That's the logic of building a mass movement as the constant task. But we try to find all loopholes that we can.

Cross and Clenched Fists

When newly arrested people ask me to draw on their bone pendant, their first choice is a clenched fist, not the bird. A reflex gesture?

Anyway, one Good Friday, I drew the same clenched fist against a cross bar. I tried to recall an appropriate quotation and mis-remembered Morley's "You have not convinced a man just because you have silenced him." Instead, I thought the quote was "You have not silenced a just man just because you have killed him."

Some detainees suggested changing "you" to "they," since those who receive our handicraft should not feel they are being accused, too. I notice that the image and the quote tend to be used for our martyrs — Bobby de la Paz, Edjop, Nilo Valerio.

Sometime back I read a theological piece by a Japanese theologian. He said Buddha's hands are fully open in resignation. Lenin's hands are clenched tight into fists. But Christ's are half-clenched or half-open. Neither absolutely resigned nor absolutely struggling.

I thought that was clever, but not quite fair to those who would be Christians in the struggle. Later, I saw it as reflecting the middle class captivity of theology, the anguish and the tension at not quite clenching the fist to fight, and accusing those who do of being less than open to the other aspects of life. On the other hand, not able to deny the need for change, and unable to simply

resign themselves. The image is also unfair to Buddha, but I leave that part of the argument to the Vietnamese Buddhists.

Anyway, I thought of painting a crucifixion, with one hand open and the other clenched into a fist. I was influenced by a poster someone drew before martial law, of an open, begging hand gradually closing into a fist. That was one of the first posters I made in Camp Olivas. I added the quotation "There is greater love in anger than in pity." The officer who interrogated me refused to let the poster through.

When I was attending a conference in France I got to thinking of the open hand and the clenched fist again. The group I was in had people working with community organizations. I thought how people are at the start — one hand open, begging for some relief from those above them, but clenched fists against each other, competing for what trickles down. At the end of the organizing process, the clenched fists are directed to their proper target, upwards. The open hands receive each other as companions in a shared struggle.

Back to the cross. The blood from the nailed hands brought to mind the persecuted Christians' message: "The blood of martyrs is the seed of new Christians." It was a natural step to make the blood flow down to become red banners.

The Forest Lives Forever

When I was barely starting to read movement literature, I was fascinated by Pomeroy's *The Forest*, with its sustained imagery. When Amado Guerrero came out with his theoretical critique of Pomeroy, I felt some sense of loss.

We were once brought to visit Taruc in Camp Panopio, and a student from Holy Spirit who had read Pomeroy asked Taruc what he thought. "Oh, he's still lost in the forest." She thought he didn't take her seriously and complained to me about it.

I said Taruc was saying something serious. He accused Pomeroy of looking only at the forest. He didn't distinguish the individual

a tree
is
born
a tree dies;
the forest
lives
forever

trees, lauan, kamagong, etc. That was the remote origin of the line: "A tree is born, a tree dies; the forest lives forever."

It's a difficult tension to handle well — the individual and the collective, the movement. We are often accused, unfairly, of not valuing the individual. But the whole struggle to change structures is precisely so that the greatest number of individual persons can develop fully.

The Pilipino translation adds another layer of meaning. "*May punong isinilang, may punong nabuwal. Nguni't patuloy ang buhay ng gubat.*" It's the tension between leaders and the movement. Leaders come and go, but we should not so stress the movement that leadership becomes "incidental." That's the populist, anarchist tendency.

Candles in the Wind

Almost one year of detention passed before I found out that the symbol of Amnesty International is a candle wrapped around with barbed wire. Before that, the image grew in my mind because I was reading Frankl's logotherapy and he had a passage "He who would give light must endure burning."

Later, feminist critique made that plural, to avoid the sexist bias. "Those who would give light, must endure burning." It must be the most requested design on our wall plaques.

I like the double allusion of "burning" — to suffer, but also to burn within. I remember two novels I read in novitiate. One, on Thomas Aquinas, was *The Quiet Light.* The other, on Augustine, was *The Restless Flame.* Initially, what attracts about activists is their dedication, their willingness to sacrifice, to give their all. But, as a poem says, changing the world is not just a matter of heart. It calls for serious thinking, which calls for some calm, keeping cool. Even cold calculations are part of it.

The term from my seminary past is *sacra indifferentia*, sacred indifference. The idea is to keep oneself as free as possible from prejudgments and preferences, so that all angles can be considered, and what is "objectively" optimum is revealed. The other image

(like Aquinas) is the quiet sense of confidence an activist has, even under fire, when he knows that the line and method is correct.

From candles and barbed wire, it's one step to candles and bars. I painted a few under the title "*Tulos Kandila.*" Reading about all the protest actions, seeing so many new faces glowing like the girls with lit candles during processions, I felt like a house-bound devotee, who has to be content with lighting a candle on the window sill as the procession passes by. I turned the lower part of the bars into candles. Procession after procession passed, reciting litanies for the release of all political prisoners. For a while, one could almost believe that the bars had turned into candles and would melt to set us free.

I sometimes allow myself to worry that some wind will snuff out our candles and leave us nothing but cold bars on our window. But we are prisoners because we did not hide our light under a bushel. We'll manage to keep burning, even in the wind.

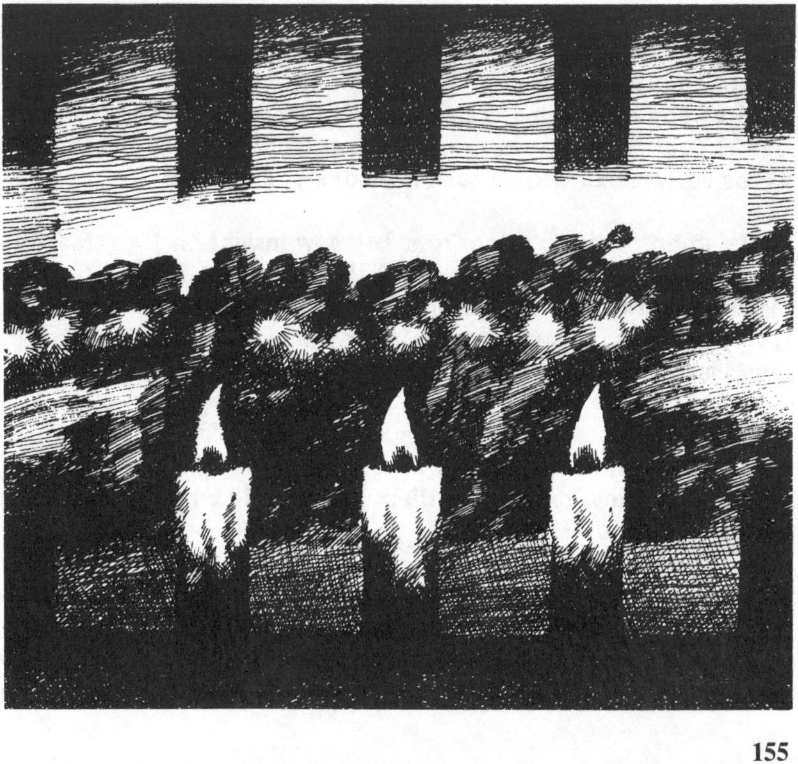

A THEOLOGY OF STRUGGLE 1983

YOU asked me to write on the parallelism between liberation theology and the emerging theology in the Philippines. Since I cannot refer to published materials, you will have to make do with the following off-the-top-of-my-head reflections.

Just before my arrest last April 1982, I remember being struck by one observation Fr. Louis Hechanova made at a theology forum — "*We should call our theology the theology of struggle, rather than a theology of liberation.*"

I think he wanted to stress the context of the emerging theology in the Philippines. The struggle for liberation is precisely that — a struggle. Not even the most sanguine activist expects liberation to come soon. The struggle is difficult and protracted.

My first impulse was to debate the point. Liberation, after all, is a process, not a one-time event only. But then I was more taken by the appropriateness of the name, not so much because it describes the current stage of the liberation process, as to emphasize the basic attitude (a key component of spirituality) that people have to come to terms with today. I remember adding that someone should write on the topic "*From Pakikisama* to *Pakikibaka*" as the cultural context of such a theology of struggle.

My mind tends to jump from any new insight back to traditional theological terms. In this case I thought of the Roman Catholic classification of the Church into triumphant (in heaven), suffering (in purgatory), or militant (on earth). Maybe some theology student can check the cultural context of that.

Anyway, militancy and struggle seem to be the emerging dominant stance of Christians in the Philippines. Whatever theology emerges as they reflect on their practice, is bound to bear the marks of such militance.

A theology of struggle, like a theology of liberation, has to start with a prior theme — *suffering.* I use this one word for the many others that are used to describe the conditions from which people need liberation and against which they struggle — poverty, op-

pression, exploitation, etc. Like struggle, suffering refers not just to an objective situation but also the subjective state of people.

In an effort to delineate the different attitudes development agencies have toward people, I proposed once the following categories: *people who suffer but do not struggle, people who suffer and therefore struggle, and people who struggle and therefore suffer.*

People who suffer but do not struggle. Why do they not struggle? This is a question with many answers. A theology of struggle must grapple with the religious aspects, perhaps better understood by citing two songs.

One is a Filipino pop hit a few years back, in the midst of martial law, Rico Puno sang:

Bakit kaya sa buhay ng tao
Mayr'ong mayama't may api sa mundo?
Kapalaran. . .
Kung hanapi'y di matagpuan
At kung minsa'y lumalapit
Nang di mo alam.*

The other song was the last song taught to me in prison before my release in April 1980:

Kay tagal ko ring nabuhay sa pantasiya;
Ang buhay raw ng tao'y kapalaran ang may pasiya,
Tulad ng gulong, mapataas, mapababa
Nguni't bakit tayo lagi na lang dukha?

Kay tagal ko ring nabuhay sa paniwalang
Kapalaran daw ng tao'y darating na lang kusa,
O ito'y ibibigay ng isang bathala
Ngunit ito pala'y isa lamang haka-haka.

*Why is it that there are rich and poor
Fate, Fortune
Seek and you won't find it
Sometimes it comes
Unexpected

Ang aking mga pangarap
Tinapon ko nang lahat;
Ang langit nating mga dukha
Tayo ang gagawa dito sa lupa!*

Here is an example of a theology that struggle against another theology that still mystifies people (I remember that even the relatives of some detainees agreed with the fatalism of Ric Puno's song). People who suffer will not struggle if they consider their suffering as their fate, willed by God. That does not seem to be too difficult or sophisticated a question for a theology of struggle or liberation, but of course it can take less crude forms.

There is a second related question or theological block. Even if people see that suffering is not fate nor God's will, they can still hesitate to struggle because of the risks involved. I do not mean the political and physical risks which are real enough. These will not be overcome by theology of whatever sort. I refer to the internal, subjective fears fed by a theology that has taught domesticating themes like these: while suffering is bad, bearing with it patiently can still save us; but if we struggle we will hate, we might kill, and that is sinful and we will end up losing more.

This warning against struggle is even stronger against armed struggle, but strongest against any struggle that involves fighting in the company of non-Christians, especially atheists.

I do not want to underestimate the complexity of conservative theological and political propaganda that dominates many people who suffer even after they have decided to struggle.But both libe-

*** Long have I lived with illusions
That life is ruled by fate
Like a wheel turning round
One is up, one is down
But why are we always poor?**

**Long have I lived believing
That fortune comes unexpected
Or bestowed by God
Ah these are all speculations**

**I've thrown my dreams away
The heaven of the poor
We will have to build
Here on earth!**

ration theology and the emerging theology of struggle in the Philippines lag behind the actual practice of Christians on these two issues, I think.

People who struggle and therefore suffer. This third phenomenon has provoked and produced the more dominant theological reflections (oral and written) today.

We should not be surprised because this is a very Christian tradition — the tradition of suffering witness, or martyrdom. It is also a very Filipino tradition, given our historical experience of a hitherto unfinished revolution and struggle.

I remember reading more than one sociologist who claim that one of the most central cultural icons of the Filipino is the suffering Messiah, who struggled to help save the people and failed. I also remember reacting to this observation and inviting fellow Christians in the early 70's to reflect on the theological and cultural breakthrough that we need to make toward the slogan "Dare to struggle, dare to win! " Instead of daring to struggle and to suffer and to lose again.

A fellow detainee reminded me that perhaps such tradition while appearing to be lacking in hope, is just right for the present stage of the struggle which is at a strategic defensive stage. We have gone beyond the earliest substage when most people who suffer do not yet struggle. At this more advanced substage most people who suffer already struggle or at least see the need to struggle, and still the over-all balance of forces is against us. No matter how many small victories accumulate as foretaste of what is to come (my seminary theology teacher told us that the more precise translation is "first-instalment"), the number of people who suffer will increase as more people struggle.

The emerging theology of struggle thus takes the form of testimonies, as our martyrs speak to us after their death in their testaments of faith. We also keep them alive through songs and poems in the midst of our tears and struggle.

Some future editors can compile these materials (I underline the fact that the materials are both written and oral) according to the needs of the communities that will emerge.

Section Five

inter(im)views

MY FIVE YEARS IN PRISON
OHD INTERVIEW 1980

I'M not bitter, If I were it would mean the last five years were senseless and without meaning, useless. I learned so many lessons, in prison and formed deep friendship. I grew, I think. It needn't have been in prison but that's where it happened. If I had been tortured badly or been kept in isolation, I'd probably feel differently.

I was never emotionally depressed for longer than a week, and then I could read or paint pictures on the walls. Once I covered a wall with paintings. The worst time was about six months after my arrest. I was in an isolation cell in Pampanga. It was hot and dusty. Moves to free me had failed and at times I thought of escaping. I worried what my old friends thought of me, now that the government was accusing me of being a communist. Would they doubt I was a priest, a Christian? Who were my friends? My past was clear but what of the future?

Some in prison became so depressed they withdrew into themselves in a pathological way. One man was badly tourtured but revealed nothing of his work or friends. But afterwards, whenever there was a confrontation with the guards — a hunger strike for our rights, for example — he would become suspicious of others, sit by himself and refuse to talk. He was anticipating further torture and couldn't face up to it.

TRINING Herrera (Mrs. Trinidad Herrera) the president of the ZOTO Tondo squatters organization was arrested and tortured and then put in with us. Unlike the other man, she had given the military some information. She was in a state of shock. The prisoners who met her put her in a circle and began to sing songs of welcome.

"I am Trining Herrera," she said, "I resign from all my involvements." She said it in such a way that the group didn't know what to do expect repeat the songs. Trining said, "I'll turn my back on you." She did as she said and she wouldn't eat or talk afterwards.

She felt a deep sense of guilt for giving the information, she told me later, and had nightmares that the people of Tondo were lynching her. I was called to talk to her and tried to explain forgiveness.

There are two ways to look at forgiveness, I told her. We can wait for the person to repent and then forgive. But if we recognize the worth of a person we forgive beforehand, then the person gets the grace of repentance.

I told her a story about a man in the movement who under torture had given information and afterwards felt guilty and worried. One night in prison he heard someone moving by his bed and thought he was going to be killed. A voice spoke close to his ear: "We are more angry at the army than you. You're still one of us. Later we'll worry about the damage you did. Now, sleep, knowing you are one with us."

We have to forgive. We are all weak. In prison you know this very well. I remember an Italian journalist who wrote of the Viet Cong cadres who lived and worked in Saigon for years before the communists took over. "I admired them," the journalist said, "because of their dedication, but I'm scared too. Would men who took such risks and made so many sacrifices understand human weaknesses when they came to power?"

You've heard the expression "wounded healer." That's what we are in prison. You have to know weakness in order to forgive and restore a person. In prison we know human limitations. Young people in the movement don't. In prison we're more tolerant and human. Don't crush the bruised reed.

Every movement has to form its leaders. In prison you are more liable to realize this takes time and will never be perfect. There's a parallel with Christ's life: after his work with the crowds in the beginning of his public life, he changed and concentrated on forming the Apostles to make sure his work would continue. Now I see the need to consciously form young people so they can grow as we did in prison. It hopefully won't be necessary for all of them to do a stint in prison. I want to do this formation work and leave the limelight and the mass actions to others.

PRISON is like a novitiate. You learn a spirituality, a spirituality for struggle. It's a time to gather yourself together as a human being. You're not worried about skills or assignments — just as in a religious novitiate — but about what you are and what is your total commitment. In prison I made my decision to be with the poor forever. I took my vows: obedience to a group that is obedient to the call of the people; creative participation, meaning you just don't implement the decisions of others, but also make suggestions and act as a subject; and thirdly, perseverance — keep struggling, that is.

The best times in prison were the evenings when we'd have long, quiet desultory talks that were often irreverent. We felt close to and comfortable with one another.

I'm grateful for the bishops who came to see me — Bishop Chi of Korea, — who was in prison himself: "Korean jails are worse," he told me — Cardinal Sin, Bishop Gaviola and others. They showed their solidarity. I think bishops who have their own priests in jail should be particularly sensitive. The priest in jail is probably someone who wasn't in close contact with the bishop before, so dialogue may be strained at first. I know I didn't talk to my own superiors much before prison. It's up to the bishop to reach out to the priest, to go more than half way to reach him.

I think we can all agree that action for justice must in one way or another stress peoples' organization and peoples' power. We should all be developing genuine local leaders whom we can point to. All the rest we can quarrel about.

We shouldn't be satisfied with saying "the people are aware." They must be organized in definite peoples' organization. Awareness must be incarnate in organization, and these organizations must be led by local leaders we can identify, talk to, evaluate, work with. This will help us avoid slogans.

Slogans come and go. Continuity will be in the local organization and its leaders and we can see how they grow. We can see if something is really being built up at the base. These local leaders, too, will become our regional and national leadership.

I'm worried about middle class leadership that has not risen from the grassroots or has not forged links with the grassroots. They will tend to be more divorced from the day-to-day life and the perceptions of the poor than leaders who have come from the villages. I have a genuine fear that a group may take advantage of all the peoples' sacrifices, install itself in power and the people remain a base only. A leader from the village will always be able to look back on his own experience of the peoples' lives — he can visit them — and so he is more anchored in the people. This is not to deny the need of broad planning and administrative skills.

We need strong local leaders rising in the movement as we need them in the villages. They are the people who can stand up and challenge the other leaders. Any leader if unchallenged will be paternalistic; he should try not to be so, but it's almost unavoidable. We need this creative tension between people and leaders. The best guarantee that we will have it is if our leadership is from the villages and not only from the middle class.

I wish I had a village base.

You can talk all you want to Church people about justice and involvement, but little will happen till they themselves meet a good farmer leader or a good union organizer and are taken by his conviction and dedication.

A leader somehow defines the organization but somehow the organization must produce a leader who truly symbolizes it. It's a two-way relationship. We need parties and a movement, but equally important are the local leaders of local organizations, the free, democratic, rooted, dedicated men and women from the villages and factories.

PRISON wasn't always serious. One day a faith healer visited us. He claimed he could remove a sore tooth by touching it with his finger. One of us with toothache volunteered. The faith healer studied the tooth carefully, then wrapped one of his fingers in a white cloth — white for Tuesday — and all of a sudden made a quick jab at the tooth with his finger. "All right," he said, "now

spit it out." The half-believing patient spat and out came the tooth. Others lined up, some old Marxists among them.

He had different handkerchiefs for different days and when he saw a bad case, would say "I'll come back on Thursday when my power is at its height."

We also had a visit from a Jesuit psychologist. All kinds of people came to see us.The Jesuit told us he would hypnotize us so that we would fly wherever we wanted to go. "Some of you will fly with your arms straight out in front of you like Superman. Others will keep your arms swept back at your sides. Ready? "

He began to talk and suddenly I felt my arms dropping to my sides, getting ready for flight. "We will burst through this ceiling," the Jesuit said, "and do some astral travelling, then we'll regroup and come back. Off we go."

I only flew around Manila, but some of us went as far as Isabela and one went to a beach in Holland.

Later we asked the Jesuit if he could teach us to levitate or bilocate — useful skills for prisoners. He couldn't. He did say that theoretically it was possible to hypnotize the guards so that they wouldn't see us if we walked out.

WE should realize that the Church and Christians will always be a minority in Asia, even in the Philippines.

It's wrong to think of the Church leading a mass movement. We are to be the leaven, the critical element, the dynamic, creative, independent voice. The temptation exists in the Philippines to forget this and to rely on the power of the Church or on its leadership. The rest of Asia where this is not at all possible because of the small numbers of Christians teaches us what our real task is.

How to be a creative minority? How to know the realities of power and not be naive? How to avoid being absorbed by power and the wish to dominate? That's the problem.

There will always be a role for the free, prophetic Christian Even if the new system is better there will still be problems and people in charge who don't like criticism. We must be prepared to speak out. We shouldn't place all our hopes in any system but be ready to criticize and to expect persecution if we work for the creative transformation of society. When I say Christians will always be a minority, I mean that, regardless of numbers, our position is not based on power but on truth. How do we create this minority?

It's important to know the uses of power so that we can be effective, but that's not what is most important. We must be credible witnesses to all of love, concern and the struggle for justice for ordinary men and women. We must be intelligent, but not tied totally to power movements. We have to relate to them but not be dominated by them.

We need a theology of the underground for all the Christians who are there. They often want to translate their Christianity into an effective force in their lives but without the traditional support, for example, the institutional Church that you have in the legal world, it is very difficult.

PRIESTS are urged to stay out of politics but what about military chaplains? In one camp they have special retreats (cursillos) that aim at getting prisoners to inform on their friends, something they refused to do under torture.

One woman leader of Manila squatters who is in her fifties was arrested during Holy Week. She is a traditional, pious person and so she went to confession and, on the urging of the priest, she told all her secrets. Later the intelligence men stripped her naked, beat her and asked questions about the very matters she had told the priest. But that's Filipino history. The revolution of 1896 was also betrayed by a priest who had knowledge from confession.

Prisoners trust the chaplains and often give them messages for their friends. Invariably these messages wind up with the intelligence men. When Church people are arrested it usually is the chaplain who first approaches them. It's for the safety of the Church

person, perhaps, but the chaplain appears like a tool of the military.

There should be some pastoral care of soldiers, but not by priests who are part and parcel of the system.

I said my first mass in prison on Christmas Eve 1974, a few weeks after my arrest. In the homily I spoke about the way my friends were tortured. The army wouldn't let me say a public mass again until 1979.

Then we often had parents of the detainees at our mass and I tried to explain the commitment of children within a Christian framework. I used Matthew 25, for example. People, both prisoners and their families — had a great liking for the story of the old woman and the judge: the old woman kept knocking and badgering the judge till he finally gave her what she wanted, not for love but simply to get rid of her. The people saw plenty of comparisons with our Martial Law set up. If the old woman could do that, how much more can God do!

You remember Berrigan's phrase "remembering — dismembering." At mass we often used it. The first mass was celebrated when Christ and the apostles were about to be arrested; it was celebration in the face of crisis. The group was about to scatter, one would betray him; they would forget their vows to one another. They met and Christ once again tried to forge their commitment, to bring them to remember their promises.

The mass therefore provides for weakness; it is a time for remembering, and it alternates with times of weakness, forgetting and scattering. The call of the mass is always to begin anew with one another, to re-vow commitment, to stick with old friends and groups even when there has been weakness and not look for new ones. Some day this group, constantly renewing itself, will be so strong, we hope, that it will not shatter under attack.

This is the season of dismemberment. No group now is strong enough to weather all attacks; they will all be dismembered. But the time of strength will come.

THE first task of a prisoner is to get out and continue the work. But in prison it's not enough to be just a prisoner. You must struggle in prison for your rights and your dignity as a person. You must struggle against self-pity and the temptation to withdraw into yourself and not care for others! You must struggle to do more, to be a more authentic person.

Your rights are yours if you exercise them. That's true inside and out. Now I move from the small prison to the bigger one.

I realize I have become somewhat of a symbol. At first I rebelled against the idea. I felt it was a burden. Others create the symbol and then they pressure you to live according to the image they have made. Later I accepted it. I don't choose to be a symbol, though in some ways because I have acted in a certain way I have co-created the symbol. I'll try to live as people want, but I won't destroy myself to do so. Sometimes I make decisions according to what I know people dear to me want.

I recognize the need for public performance; at a high mass you must be solemn. In public I'll act as required; in small groups of friends I'll be more myself.

Some people thought I wanted to stay in prison as a symbol. For some people it may be a vocation, but I'm for changing the symbolic prisoner.

I want to help set up genuine pluralism in the movement, especially among Christians. Some Christians in the movement can be members of parties but they must also be able to meet as Christians with others to develop their faith. Other Christians can share the goals of parties, but will not be linked organizationally, while others can have some loose organizational connection. All these people who value their Christian faith must be able to share with one another in order to strengthen each other and understand each other. If we don't, our Christian life will be lost. For our purposes the bond will be Christ, not ideology. One of the things we can do, for example, is study Marx and others as *Christ-*

ians. Right now that isn't being done; Christianity's role in the struggle is being defined mainly by outsiders.

I'm for everything that speaks of freedom, for the individual and the group. We can't coerce people. We have to provide options suitable to the needs of people which vary so much. The movement can't be monolithic and hope to succeed. We can't succeed if there's no place in the movement for people like Bishops Labayen and Claver. Every sincere person is welcome.

I notice in the movement many trends towards pluralism and greater people's participation. I'm very hopeful.

We shouldn't accept people on the condition that they change. We should be content that they share our program goals, for example, an end to Martial Law, an end to feudalism and imperialism.

SOME people such as Karl Levin (Democrat Senator of Michigan who visited me in prison and worked for my release) say that I am naive in hoping that some constructive relationship can be worked out between Christians and the left. I have to admit that the burden of proof is with me, especially if we look at the lessons of history. But I cannot take the traditional Catholic position that there is no hope for a united front. I don't pretend to speak for all Catholics, I don't claim to have mastered Christianity. I feel, however, that what I do is acceptable within the Catholic tradition; it's an acceptable, valid option among those open to Catholics. Above all I tell people, don't apologize for your Christianity or other ideas that some people in the movement may not agree with. How can the movement in the Philippines be truly nationalistic if there is no distinct Filipino Christian voice?

Christianity must never be merely a tool. We shouldn't say as one theologian said once — he's changed since then — that he does theology only because it's useful in the struggle. That's not finding your real self-identity or gathering yourself as a human being. You must do theology because it's what you believe in. If we Christians are not completely one with ourselves there will be no creative Christianity or honest dialogue with Marxism.

I want to study what happens to the beliefs and thinking of the local leaders as they engage in the struggle. What roles does Christianity play? I think that work to develop local leaders is the most important task, otherwise the leaders of the movement will be all middle class, and if some poor people rise up in the movement without proper development, they will be corrupted. The formation of the true local leader — the free and committed leader — is the basis of the success of our work.

Committees of elites can become monsters. Who will control the intelligence apparatus that will have to be set up someday, as in any society, so that it doesn't become the power behind the scenes? Our only hope is the presence of strong leaders who have risen from the people at every level of the movement. If they ask me what job I want later, I'll say, ombudsman.

On November 1st in prison we decided to list all our friends who had been killed. We put up four big pieces of paper and each of us wrote down the names we remembered. The 30 of us listed 270 people. This didn't include the thousands of small, anonymous farmers and others who have been killed.

Most of us, I'm afraid, have no spiritual or interior life. We must stress recollection or gathering of oneself. If we don't, we're too tied to external activity and become inflexible slaves. If we have a spiritual life, we know who we are and where we are and what we're about: we can smile at the guards.

There are two tendencies. One is to throw oneself completely into action, forgetting to form one's own inner life or spirituality as if that were a luxury. The other is to have a radiant serenity, like a Buddhist, but not worry about changing society. I think we should do both; develop ourselves as human beings as we work for liberation. Otherwise we're not convincing witnesses. People will say "We like your cause, but look what it has done to you as a person."

But to pray and build this interior life, we need a community. It can't be just the traditional religious community, because it was geared to form people for a stable way of life, where now the need is to form people who are mobile, who can reflect on the run. We

need a new spirituality or else we're vulnerable and weak in the face of opposition. By spirituality I mean sense of wholeness and direction. That's what liberation is about, I think, a wholeness at every level, from the individual up to the whole society. We'll have different jobs but if we have this wholeness we'll have the same stance.

The choice is sometimes presented between the strong, lonely man and the person who ties his identity completely to that of the group. Both aspects are needed, but I think hitherto we have emphasized the former. Yet even the strong and lonely man needs a community.

The man of wholeness who is able to withdraw, to reflect, who has, as they say, silent spaces, shows coolness in crisis. Life's situations have a way of coming together and making sense for him in the way that a poem finally fits together in the poet's mind. Whatever he is doing he knows he's making revolution even if he is just arranging cars and apartments. He is able to relate small things to bigger events. He's less selfish. He knows he has value independent of his achievements. Wholeness clarifies the basic ideological standpoint: for whom do we struggle, with whom?

Without this wholeness we're weak under torture. Why do some break under torture? Perhaps they never felt full participation in a group and the knowledge that others would suffer the same for them.

Church people shouldn't look for perfection in action groups or people's organizations. Even if the poor are struggling for justice, they will not be perfectly just themselves. There's always sin. If we wait for the perfect group to support, we will postpone our involvement or we'll support a group we think is ideal and later be disillusioned. We'll feel betrayed and used, but it's our rosy hopes that created the disillusionment in the first place.

The poor in their efforts at justice are substantially good and decent; that should be enough for us. Surely they have more right on their side than the oppressors. Live with the faults of the poor: let the wheat and weeds grow. There's more wheat than weeds.

Someday there'll be time for the harvest and evaluation of what we've done. We must be patient. We've been patient with our old apostles for hundred of years.

My hopes for the future? I think that soon we'll find that the villages will have their peoples' organizations with good local leaders who are sophisticated enough to make alliances and handle national issues.

If we talk of basic change in the economic and political structures and a new and transformed presence of the Church, well, that'll be a longer time. But, I hope to see it in my lifetime. That's another reason I'm not bitter. This is an informed hope, a realistic one, I think I can give a reasoned basis for what I say. I'm not unique. If I can change so much, why not others?

In prison I often thought what would I shout if I were going to be shot. Long live the people? The movement? Church? Christ? I thought and thought and decided it would be "long live the struggle," since that includes everything.

"WE MUST TRANSFORM STRUCTURES" INTERVIEW WITH BREAK THROUGH (revised) 1980

I think we, middle class Christians, have similar values and starting points, I used to just look into myself, read myself, speak out, and people would think I had been observing them. They'd ask, "Ed, how did you know I was like that? " And I'd answer, "No, that was me I was talking about."

I'm like you in many ways. Church background, middle class upbringing, worldview and theology. A lot of dilemmas and questions I faced, I found out were also confronting others like you.

One of the pamphlets I wrote was the *Passion, Death and Resurrection of the Petty-Bourgeois Christian.* In fact, I consider that the central paradigm of my political and theological development. I really went through the anguish of the middle class who want to get involved, but feel torn between two choices that are both extreme. One favorite image was Christ on the cross, crucified between two thieves, the left and the right. The one on the right steals economic resources by exploitation. The one of the left steals political power by totalitarianism. Christ in the middle represented the Christian choice, which also got labelled the Filipino choice, the Third World choice, the human choice. Essentially, however, it is the middle class choice. It is not bad *per se.* In fact, it is a legitimate choice. What I refuse to accept is the effort of those who want to sanctify it by saying it is the only authentic Christian choice. It's more accurate to call it the middle class Christian choice.

During our time, activist Christians wanted to be radical. This was partly because of the various pronouncements of church leaders and thinkers who said that Christianity is more radical than the most radical ideology. Anyway, under the influence of Marxist literature, to be radical got identified in our minds with being proletarian. Since we were of middle class origin and status, that meant we had to adopt a proletarian standpoint, to make what others called a class choice. This led to downgrading of the middle class. We confused the question of our own class transformation

from middle class to proletarian with the question of the middle class's own distinct and legitimate participation, as middle class, in the struggle.

There is reason, of course, for the observation that the middle class is vacillating and unable to lead the revolution. But this doesn't mean it cannot be part of it. You don't have to be proletarian to make revolution. It helps, but you don't have to be. You can be perfectly middle class and be a member of the National Democratic Front. But since young people want to commit themselves totally, they also want to get away from the image of the middle as *segurista* and hesitant. So, they seek transformation into proletarians, so they can be part of the vanguard, the leadership. There's nothing wrong with such a choice, but it should not lead to condemning these who remain middle class. There are revolutionary middle class people.

Besides, transformation is not such an easy and quick process. It involves some dying. Some talk of class suicide. It can take the form of rejecting one's middle class family and social circles. Sometimes, the negative part is given more attention — the rejection, the anger. But transformation is not just that. In fact, one sign that transformation has basically happened is when the middle class-turned proletarian can accept those who remain middle class, and has the patience and understanding to establish united front relations with them.

The middle class people have their own pretensions, of course. They say that both extremes are imperfect, both left and right. *Virtus in medio.* They set up straw targets, caricatures. Thus, one side is accused of emphasizing too much spirituality; the other is accused of emphasizing too much materialism. Then the middle class proclaims: "We have both." Actually, when they attack the left for being too materialist, they mean mechanical materialism, while the right is attacked for its idealism. Being in the middle is to be balanced, to be all-sided, rather than one-sided. That is supposed to be dialectical materialism, but the middle claims it as its own. But I know some people on the left give the middle class reason to think that way, because they also misinterpret materialism as mechanical and crude, undialectical.

On Imperfections in the Movement

To get involved politically is to enter into a relationship that is far from perfect. Actually, the same is true of personal relationships, and I've learned to draw insights from one to apply to the other.

To make a Christian choice, however, is associated with making a perfect choice. We are not trained to make Christian choices among imperfect alternatives. There is a temptation, therefore to postpone choice, or avoid it altogether. You wring your hands, saying both left and right are alike, and wait for Godot.

So what happens? Either you make a choice, but based on the illusion that you have chosen a perfect movement, a perfect organization, with perfect methods and perfect leaders. And when people in the organization prove to be only too human, when they commit mistakes, when the political line turns out to be less than perfect, you get disillusioned. You say: "I was deceived! " You leave, only to search for the really perfect organization. Like the perfect boy or girl. Maybe this time. . .

During the pre-martial law days, there were those who didn't want the KM (Kabataang Makabayan), and therefore transferred to the SDK (Samahang Demokratikong Kabataan). When they did not want that either, they transferred to 3KP (Kilusang Kristiyano ng Kabataang Pilipino). They find that it is not perfect either. So they leave it and look for another.

With this attitude, you either wait forever and never get involved, or you get cynical after discovering that organizations you join are not perfect. But remember, you're dealing with people who are also undergoing transformation even as they seek to transform society.

I am not saying that we should be liberal and say, all are human, all are imperfect. It is correct that we should look for basic *minima.* All I want to stress is that even if a political line that an organization carries is basically correct, it is not perfect. Besides, even if a line is correct, the methods of work might not be. Or the methods might be OK, but there's something wrong with the style of work.

A movement for change involves a lot of people at various levels of development. You've heard of "uneven development." Some would consider it a general law of change. You set standards, you set ideals. You have the right to expect everyone to strive to reach them, but do not demand perfection.

On Being a Priest

I allow myself to claim some success as a priest on two grounds — liturgical, and ecumenical.

Liturgy is associated with priesthood. As I understand it, liturgy comes from two Greek words: *laos*, meaning people, and *ergon*, meaning work. Given these two root words, you can have two translations of liturgy, with opposite emphasis. Laos-ergon can be translated as "public works," and liturgy is like a project done by those in power, using the money of the people to keep them from being restless.

The opposite translation is laos-ergon as "mass action." Mass action is usually from below and directed against those in power. It is democratic, but can also be disorganized. It is very alive, and expresses the spontaneous sentiments of the participants. In liturgy as mass action, we do not go to mass (as if it were the priest's mass and we merely witness a performance); we celebrate mass. It is something we ourselves do.

In liturgy, as in mass actions, there are two aspects we both have to pay attention to. One is small group liturgy, parallel to discussion groups. The other is the big, public liturgy, parallel to the demonstrations. After Vatican II, experimentations on new liturgies tended to be only small-group efforts, house liturgies. But they never got out to the streets.

On the other hand, let's take a look at demonstrations. I found the relationship between Plaza Miranda and Quiapo church quite symbolic. There would be two liturgies going on. Inside Quiapo church, it was dark and mysterious. Only the priest spoke. There was mystification and domestication of people. Outside, at Plaza Miranda, they would be gathering to discuss the issues of the day, shouting their protest and celebrating their struggle. I always

felt that we should be able to have liturgies like that, and not just the one inside the church.

During the Holy Week of 1972, we tried to hold a public liturgy on Good Friday — "The Passion, Death and Resurrection of Juan de la Cruz." We ended in Plaza Miranda. Some bystanders misunderstood and criticized us for holding a political rally on such a holy day! It was a big crowd, about 3000 to 4000 people. The rites couldn't be spontaneous. We had to have a script for our street play and the various stops.

In big mass actions and liturgies, in the Plaza Miranda crowd, practically everyone belonged to a smaller group that had met beforehand in face-to-face discussion groups. The DGs are the small-group liturgies. But you can't remain at that level only. You need to mass together in bigger numbers, for public acts. In this bigger, public act, you need not know everyone personally. Also, you can't have just anyone doing or saying what he or she pleases. There is leadership, set speakers, although you try to maximize mass participation through songs and chants and other actions.

The other ground (ecumenical) refers to the concept of the priest as mediator. I can best explain this in relation to my work for a united front.

On Filipino Marxists

Marxists in the Philippines will try to gain as many adherents as possible. But it is a realistic thesis to say that they will remain a minority. The last publicly claimed membership of the CPP is 30,000.

To be a minority does not mean to be isolated. A minority can present a program and have it accepted by the majority. In the CPP's case, it is the national democratic program that they offer to the people for majority support and participation in implementing it. This ND program is a political program. It is not an ideology. An ideology, or worldview, is more comprehensive.

I think the revolution will be waged successfully, even if Marxists are only a minority in the Philippines. My position is that

there will also be a conscious group of Christian national democrats. They are Christian in their worldview; they have revolutionized their understanding of Christianity. But its incarnation in an actual political program is the national democratic program. Not because this was formulated by Christians or because you can find it in the Bible. But because it is the application of their basic impulse to love and serve their neighbor in the most effective way possible, according to the deepening insights of people as they progress.

We must transform structures. But to do this, we must use whatever accomplishments people have achieved throughout the years. That, for me, is a basic Christian attitude and approach for living in this world.

On Christianity and Marxism

When you discuss Christianity and Marxism, you discuss ideology. I don't encourage that level of discussion as a starting point. But it is a trap used often by social democrats, since it serves their purpose. They want talk to remain at the level of ideology, where agreement is next to impossible, instead of focusing on political lines and programs, where Christians and Marxists can unite and cooperate.

For me, the first question should be this: Can one be a Christian and a national democrat at the same time, even though the national democratic program was formulated by Marxists, applying Marxism to Philippine society, and not by Christians?

Here you are. You are a Christian. You understand your faith as demanding that you love, not just individuals, but groups, classes, a whole people. To do that, you accept the need to engage in social action, in political action. You want to be part of the forward movement of mankind toward the coming Kingdom. Your problem is this: What specific shape will the society you seek to bring about take — economically, politically, culturally?

In the Catholic tradition, it used to be simple. You read the Papal encyclicals like *Rerum Novarum and Quadragesimo Anno*, and similar documents that identified the Christian alternative as

Christian democracy. Part of being Christian is that it is formulated by Christians.

Before 1971, various Christian groups in the Philippines, like the FFF and CSM were content with accepting the program of the encyclicals, and even adapted them to the Philippines. Then the ND program burst into the scene, especially with the First Quarter Storm. But the way it came across, then, to be a national democrat was equivalent to being a Marxist. Not even ND organizations like the KM clearly distinguished political program from ideology.

We had a hard time. On the one hand, we were already dissatisfied with reformism. It simply was not working. Our dissatisfaction was based more on experience than any theoretical critique. For example, by the time martial law was declared in 1972, there were 70 unsolved agrarian cases in one small province alone. Tenants were being harassed by armed guards. Some were being killed. Even the peasants were telling us that reformism wasn't working.

We said we should be radical. But to be radical, then, was first understood as being Marxist. But we wanted to remain Christian. That was our dilemma.

What we had to do was first to dissociate Christianity from its identification with a specific reformist program, which was traditionally believed to be the Christian political program. At that time, we were helped by Metz, with his political theology.

Metz identified two stages of Christian political theology. The first was the identification of Christianity with a particular political order, as in feudalism. As a reaction to this, Christianity became apolitical under capitalism, either concentrating on the interpersonal sphere of human relations, or saying "All systems are imperfect in the light of the Kingdom." It seemed pretty progressive, but in effect, it accepted the existing system, at least by default. In practice, it accepted capitalism even more actively, by warning against alternative, socialist, systems and condemning these as un-Christian.

It is true that the Kingdom is not yet. We should not call any system as the absolute choice for Christians. But the Kingdom is also already here, somehow. This cannot be identified arbitrarily. One system can be judged as objectively advancing mankind ahead of another system. Metz says you must make a provisional, but not arbitrary choice. Provisional, in the light of the Kingdom (the so-called "eschatological reserve") but not arbitrary. What will be your basis for choosing? Not the Bible, not church declarations, but a rigorous examination of what really advances the liberation of mankind. Here's where social science and other sciences enter, including the question of Marxism.

Sometime later, this line of reasoning got criticized as inadequate. Latin American theologians said that Metz' position was still implicitly liberal. Why? Because the choice he advocates is only provisional. You do not really commit yourself totally to it. How can you ask someone to risk everything, including life, for something provisional? It's like saying: "You are my girl friend, tentatively." If a Christian must choose to pour his love into something, it must be seen as worth his all. I remember a nun trying to resolve this by saying: "What I choose to give myself to is imperfect. I have no illusions that it is perfection. But it is in this and through this that I commit myself to perfection."

On the Possibility of Fusion

I still have to meet the theologian or the Marxist who can put the two together. There should be no liberalism here, no easy fusion of Christianity and Marxism. No, let's give each one its due authenticity. I don't think Christianity and Marxism, theoretically and institutionally (like party and church), can be wedded. I would be the last to advocate or claim a fusion.

The united front is something else. That can and should be. The united front is based on a common program, a common incarnation, if you will. I think of the WCC slogan: "Action unites, doctrine divides." Actually, it's not that neat. The united front unites not just on the basis of action, but also on the basis of some doctrine. But full doctrinal unity is not demanded.

Ideologically, you are a Christian, politically, you are a national democrat. Somebody else is also politically a national democrat, but ideologically a Marxist. But, of course it is not static. You do not remain so cleanly distinct forever. As you continue to struggle as a Christian, for national democracy, you ask yourself: "What contribution does my being Christian give? " You think of certain values that seem to be part of Christian teaching, like individual wholeness, or importance given to small, face-to-face groups. On the other hand, these might be more middle class rather than specifically Christian.

You also identify what comes in from outside your Christian tradition, like rigorous social analysis — "concrete analysis of concrete conditions." You study Marxist class analysis, both the product and the process, the method. Once you grasp the method, you tend to apply it not just to analyzing Philippine society, but also the church, and finally, your faith. Just as you ask about the origins of imperialism and feudalism, yoiu also ask: "Where did my concepts of God come from? Of Christ? Of salvation? " You ask what sustains them. You ask yourself if they act as prod or brake to your involvement. That is when your theological concepts undergo passion and death. Some will resurrect. Others will not.

On the Serious Study of Marxism

We have to study Marxism seriously if we are to analyze Philippine society. But we should also study it to analyze our worldview. We should not be afraid to subject our theological and religious concepts to questions like: "Where do they come from? From what experience? What is their relevance? Do they hold us back from commitment? Do they push us on? "

There was a certain point when some of us were worried: "We're losing our old concepts. What will happen? " Our theology and religious identity were battered, and we felt there would be a death experience. We didn't want to die, because we were not clear about what would happen afterwards. After death, there can be resurrection. But there can also be dying that is withering away.

In other words, you outgrow certain categories. (When I was a child, I spoke like a child). You start employing secular categories,

descriptive and analytical categories. No more theology. The problem is that people want the resurrection to happen even before they die. They want to know the new theology, before letting go of the old.

There was a certain point when my theology was reduced to the biblical passage: "If you risk your life for my sake, you'll find it. But if you hold on to it, then you'll lose it." I was interpreting it in very personal terms. If I simply hold on to my theology, and refuse to go through the rigors of dialectical materialist analysis, that might just be the way to insure its loss. Because when dialectical materialism finally becomes my world view (due to its usefulness in the struggle), then my understanding of faith remains identified with idealism and mechanical materialism.

The Church in the National Democratic Society

In its best sense, the church's hold on people is ultimately ideological, not material or organizational. But just as Marxism gets incarnate in a party, so Christianity whether radical or not, must get incarnate in some organizational form. We have to think of alternative institutional forms also for the church. That is theologically acceptable and politically necessary.

There is no detailed NDF program for the alternative church in the Philippines. That is one of the reasons why many think that after the ND revolution, churches will be abolished. (The other reason is the confusion about national democracy and Marxism). In the Revolutionary Guide for Land Reform drafted by the CPP, there is a provision that sets aside land for religious purposes. That's a graphic argument for having religious institutions in the ND society.

One of the questions usually asked by the church about the ND society is this: "Will there be religious freedom? " The most immediate meaning of this is freedom of worship. When the NDF or the CPP says "Yes," the church asks further: "How do we know? Perhaps you are referring only to private worship. We want public worship." If we probe deeper into the guarantees that the church wants, we realize that for the church, the freedom to worship is tied closely to ownership of the places of worship. Even if

we take this concept of freedom, the provision in the CPP Guide for Land Reform is a sign that church ownership is recognized.

But of course, we need to come up with more features of the alternative church. We need to go even into economic aspects. For example, will the priests receive salaries from government, as a recognition that they are socially necessary, even if not productive? Or will they be supported by the free contributions of the communities they serve? Will they have to engage in productive work themselves, like St. Paul did?

Part of the responsibility of those who would change structures is to come up at least with outlines of the alternative. We cannot rest content with pointing out what's wrong with the existing structures and calling for their removal. To be revolutionary involves creation, not only destruction. We cannot rely on spontaneity, as if the new structures will arise by themselves or by the grace of the Holy Spirit. If we discuss the details of the alternative church, that is proof that we take freedom of religion seriously. After all, the target of the ND movement is not religion *per se*, but only colonial and feudal religion.

Of course, religious freedom is more than economic and political arrangements for the church. It means theology, preaching, church involvement in society. It would be wrong to give up the insights about the social dimension of faith just because society has been transformed into a less unsatisfactory one.

Need I reassure you that there is room for Path Two (Philippine Association of Theologically Trained Women) in the ND society? But I will also assure you that there will be struggle. You will be criticized and challenged to prove your social relevance and your service to the people. But whoever wanted a soft, easy role anyway? It is a very poor Christianity that cannot handle struggles.

On Facing the Organized Masses

Even the present government is easier to deal with than an awakened people. The government can be criticized as reactionary, etc. But when it is the people themselves who are raising questions like: "What added dimensions does Christianity give? What ques-

tions does it raise that are valid? What answers? ", that is more scary. To answer the people, we must hold fast to the orientation that Christianity and theology are meant to serve the liberation of the people above all. They are not primarily concerned with serving institutional interests or the identity and role of Christians in society. The interests of the broader community come first.

When Christian national democrats are confronted by the organized masses, some might feel like running away or conceding, "I'm not Christian anymore." That is a dangerous form of cowardice. Even if you are considered partly reactionary there is a place for you in the struggle. What matters is that you are principally progressive. This is where the ecumenism I referred to earlier comes in. We must unite, even if we don't agree on everything. But this is easier said than done. We're not used to united front relations. We prefer to be accepted totally or rejected totally, to love or hate thoroughly.

What we have to learn is that in this world, we are not going to face perfectly lovable people and we have to work with people who do not agree on everything. The need is to learn how to handle what is principal and secondary. Is unity principal and struggle secondary? Or is it struggle that is principal and unity secondary?

On the Charge of Being Used

Question: Some people are saying that the movement is using or exploiting religion to meet its own ends. Does the movement believe that the end justifies the means? Would you say that this is a very amoral or even immoral ethic?

"Exploiting" is an emotionally laden term. I would rather rephrase the questions: "Is the movement using religion for its political ends? " Yes. Because the movement is a political movement, it will use whatever advances its politics.

That brings up a question I used to be asked a lot. "But won't we be used? " I would answer: "If you're useful, you will be used. If you are not used, you better start worrying. You might be useless! " I was half-joking, of course. There is a way of "being used" by the movement that does not offend your dignity. For example,

an organization might recruit you because of your talent such as writing, or because you can raise funds, or because of your influence in the church. Of course, that is not the only reason you are being recruited, but it is part of the reason.

Does the movement use religion to advance political ends? Yes. Does the end justify the means? That is an often misunderstood question of classical theology. It was meant to prevent moral ends from being invoked to justify intrinsically immoral means. But it does not mean that ends cannot justify means. For example, there are means that are called morally indifferent or neutral. According to some thinkers, killing *per se* might be neutral (this is disputed by others). Morally neutral means can be justified only by their ends. If you kill in defense of your violated sister, or in a just war (extended now to just revolution), it is a morally defensible act. Of course, there is an *ad hominem* argument also. Those who worry about the left using religion for its purposes do not ask the same questions of those who use religion for "right" ends.

You ask if the movement is amoral? No, it is a very moral movement. It is fighting for justice and its members are generally driven by deep motives of sacrifice and service. But, of course, the movement and its members have weaknesses, and commit mistakes.

On the Exercise of Democracy

When the movement gets people to join organizationally, anyone who feels that he or she is being used has a right to complain. But the right won't be there unless it is exercised. Some merely grumble in private, but do not confront people in authority. They don't assert their democratic rights. They are afraid of confrontation, of struggle; they keep their feelings to themselves. Because of this, leaders will tend to think that everything's OK. Then, suddenly, things break down.

But is your leader all-knowing? Where does a leader's correct ideas come from? From theoretical readings alone? Don't we say that correct ideas ultimately come from practice?

The training of leaders in the exercise of democracy also involves the training of members in the exercise of their democratic rights. We face a lot of problems in this matter. We come from institutions (family, church, school) where we survive, by not exercising our democratic rights. We hide our true feelings and ideas to avoid being punished. It is true that we try to build a democratic movement, but many of us (shall I say most of us?) are used to evading, rather than confronting authority? We do have the advantage of a political line and methods of work that are known by members, and not just by leaders. That is a clear basis for criticizing leaders. Anyway, you can always exercise your ultimate right to secede, to resign.

In general, the exercise of democracy is still weak. That is why there is frequent talk about "being used." Usually it comes from allies who waver after some involvement. But the idea is to "use" someone while explaining why and what for. As you understand more, you want to be used some more. You also want to use others, in a good sense. We are supposed to be able to use each other. I don't mean only politically. There is emotional support we need from each other.

Part of growing up and deepening commitment in the movement is realizing the complexity of motives among its members. Dialectics enters here, in the need to classify principal and secondary motives. Why are we here? We say, "To serve the people." What else? "To fight imperialism and fascism." What do we seek to establish? "True democracy." All these are true. But there can be secondary motives, personal motives that include self-fulfillment and other psychological needs. These can become principal, if we don't watch out.

On Lessons From Prison

It was only in Bicutan that I got this insight into the mass: The first mass was celebrated by Christ and his disciples at a time when they were about to be raided and arrested. We usually don't look at mass as a pre-arrest ceremony. We think of it as a relaxed, happy celebration. But mass was first held at a moment of impending crisis, principally from an external cause — a military

raid. But, more painfully, there was also internal crisis. One of the group had turned against it, had betrayed it.

What is the lesson for us? We played on the words of Christ: "Remember." Not merely repeat, but remember. This supposes that there will be forgetting. That there will be dismembering. The group that Christ had sought to temper will be hit from outside, will be dispersed, will break up. They will forget the principles they pledged to keep. Organizationally and ideologically, they will be broken.

What to do about it? We tend to make one of two choices. We can turn cynical, give up further effort. Or start a new group, refusing to consider working again with the old. For us in prison, the lesson, however, is that we must learn to regroup and re-commit ourselves to principles we might forget for a while. We need not seek a totally new group that starts with fresh commitments to totally new principles.

The movement has passed through many cycles of being dismembered and remembering. It did not react to being dismembered by leaving all the dispersed members to themselves and starting with totally new forces. If we do that, we'll never learn because we start always with inexperienced people. For the foreseeable future, we cannot form groups so strong and consolidated that they will not undergo forgetting and being dismembered in the face of crisis.

Now is the season of being dismembered and remembering, of forgetting and remembering. This is how we get tempered. We will eventually reach a stage when we will be so tempered that if others seek to break us, it is they who will shatter and not us. But that is a long way off. At present, any group in the movement that gets a direct hit, will shatter. The enemy is still stronger. The movement has many weaknesses.

I want to stress this lesson repeatedly. It is the only way to avoid our initial romantic tendency to start with people who haven't shown weakness yet (because they haven't been tested by crisis), and to look for new people whenever we're disappointed with the old people we started working with. Think of a married

couple who quarrel but remain committed to each other. Such commitment might be less romantic, but it is more mature. It will last. The other kind will burst like a soap bubble because it is based on an illusory desire for perfect partnership. At this stage, especially, the movement is not perfect; it is not always OK.

That's why I sometimes talk about preferring "battered" people. People who struggle despite being battered — they are more tempered. If you are not yet battered, I don't wish that you'll get battered soon! But remember, just in case that happens, that you can take time to recover — a few days, a few weeks perhaps. But the point is to recover! Don't sulk forever, saying "I want out. I was deceived. My youthful idealism was exploited!"

We will feel exploited at one time or another. We are not expecting a perfect Messiah who comes in from outside. The alternative to the present system is born within it. It bears the traces and influences, the imperfections of the existing system. Look at Christ's experience. Out of only 12 apostles, one turned out to be a Judas. His secondliner, Peter, vacillated. I think the two hotheads, the "leftist" brothers James and John must have run away farthest! But the point is to come back, once you've recovered your senses, even if somewhat shame-faced.

Three Generations

I share these thoughts with you, feeling like a grandfather with his grandchildren. You are the third generation. Our batch was the first generation of SCM who crossed the boundaries into revolutionary commitment. The second generation was the SCM that lived under martial law. They were confused about being 3KP or SCM. Politically, you are the third generation, since you have asserted SCM as a legal organization without loss of commitment to the people's struggle. See how rapid is the turnover? I'm 36 now, but I started late, at 21. That means only 15 years. Within those years, three political generations have come to be. *Sana, bilis-bilisan ninyo!* [Speed it up!]

REPRESSION

and

ON CHURCHES, POLITICS AND ART
PNF INTERVIEW 1985

A. On Theology and the Churches

1. Is it correct to say that the theology of liberation (TL) is a "liberation of theology"? On the other hand, critics seem to imply that the concept translates into a theology of (unChristian) violence.

There is no single theology of liberation; only theologies. But certain key aspects are common to all these theologies. First of all, a theology of liberation can exist only if there is a process of liberation that it can reflect on. Praxis is primary, both chronologically and epistemologically. A more systematic reflection on this praxis, both to justify it in religious (especially biblical) terms, and also to criticize it (in the original meaning of critique) — this is what I understand by a theology of liberation.

That TL is also a liberation of theology can be understood in two senses. One is that theology is liberated from "false burdens" particularly the formulation and evaluation of political lines by trying to draw political lines directly from theology (usually a variant of social democracy or anarchism). The other liberation is from theology's function as primarily serving the existing (dis) order. There is no question that TL's bias and the principal source of reactions against it is its "preferential option" for the poor in their struggle.

I don't think TL advocates violence. I still have to read a TL that does that. What riles TL's critics is that TL does not summarily condemn violence, or more precisely, armed struggle when waged by a popular movement for liberation. I should add, though, that most of the TL I have read tends to criticize violence, even when it takes the form of counter-violence against existing institutional, repressive violence.

Perhaps what an Anglican priest wrote me is more representative of the mainstream TL. He said that "revolutionary violence might not be justifiable, but it is certainly forgiveable."

2. How serious is the division of opinion in the Philippine churches today? In the Christian church, in general?

In general, just about as serious as the divisions within the societies they are part of. Of course, the churches have their own leadership who may be more or less skilled than the political leaders in handling conflicts. Also, the mechanisms of conflict resolution inside the churches are somewhat different from those in society at large. If we use political categories, I would estimate that "left" forces within the church tend to be smaller compared to the "left" in society as a whole. Also, the churches prefer to mute some of their internal conflicts for the sake of presenting a united facade to the public.

3. Are there significant differences in the way Protestants and Catholics perceive liberation theology? What about the future of ecumenism? Will it be the final saving grace of the Christian faith?

I can speak only about the circles I moved in. Protestants whom I've met tend to be more liberal than Catholics and address certain social issues and theological themes a bit ahead of Catholics. On the other hand, there is greater struggle among Catholics to arrive at a common, authoritatively binding teaching. Protestants allow more leeway for individual interpretation.

As for ecumenism, the rate of working unities and even theoretical convergence is much faster among the rank and file who meet in social action. It is much lower at the top, among church leaders. The agenda below is also less intra-church or doctrinal, but more about the church's presence in the world and in the people's struggle.

For both Protestants and Catholics, the ecumenical question that is more important is the relationship between Christianity and other religions especially Islam and Animism as operative in the Moro and Cordillera people's struggle. Expanding the scope of

ecumenism would include the encounter between Christianity and Marxism, and between both of them and nationalism.

4. How, and when, did the concept of liberation theology take root in the Philippines? Was there already evidence of this even when church elements were being referred to as "clerico-fascists?"

Theological justification and critical reflection on the social involvement of church people and Christian lay people always accompanied their praxis. Whether that would qualify as TL is hard to judge. Perhaps it is safer to say No, since a lot of the concepts and methods of theologizing were still along Western European lines. TL, especially as method, is a critical break with such theology.

I personally relied first on the so-called "political theology" of some Western European theologians to help me work out my theology. I got to read Latin American theologians only in 1972, long after my involvement in the people's struggles.

5. "The revolution will never succeed in the Philippines because Filipinos are predominantly Christians, and they will reject a foreign, godless ideology that seeks to impose an alien faith and an alien political system upon them." How do you react to this opinion?

With a smile! Even if we concede the premises of the opinion — the religiosity of Filipinos (which, by the way, need not be Christian) and the irreligiosity of Marxism and the CPP — the conclusion about the revolution not succeeding does not follow. No Marxist or CPP member claims that the main content and character of the current revolutionary process is anything other than national liberation and democracy. There is nothing irreligious or alien about that.

My next reaction is to argue from praxis. The advance of the revolutionary movement appears to be steady. This means that there is both popular support for it and, most important, popular participation in it. The revolutionaries, including the Marxists among them, must be doing something right. That is unless you buy the line that people are just being duped or terrorized. I don't think they are.

6. Do you foresee, and would you want to see, a Nicaragua-type of church-state relationship for the Philippines, in the event that the movement comes to power?

A Nicaragua-type relationship has many aspects. First of all, the presence of church people in the cabinet and other government positions need not occur here. What happened in Nica is peculiar to that country. There was a lack of qualified personnel for certain levels of government, I think we have enough lay people in the Philippines for all levels of administration.

What about the widespread support by rank and file church people and lay people for the Sandinistas? Something similar could develop here, depending on the political maturation of the revolutionary united front, and also depending on the progress of conscientization and political involvement of church and lay people.

A third element is the political hostility of the hierarchy (the bishops) to the FSLN, even though they did withdraw support from Somoza toward the end of his rule. I don't think our Catholic hierarchy will be as solidly hostile to a revolutionary regime. Of course much depends on the regime's policies and the bishops' own development. Like the Nicaraguan bishops, I expect that they will, in the main, withdraw support from the present regime, without necessarily endorsing a revolutionary alternative. More probably, they would prefer a non-revolutionary alternative, if it had any chance at all. But a growing minority among them would not find it difficult to live with a revolutionary regime.

7. Christianity in this country is described as highly ritualistic and in terms of worldview, retains much of the original colonial religion: this refers to "folk Catholicism." What can and ought to be changed? What can be adapted to present-day needs and realities?

I have done little direct study into this, and can only refer you to the rich experience of those who worked along the lines of basic Christian communities. Of course, Ileto's studies into popular religious consciousness, especially among the peasantry should give us some indication of the potential and limitations of popular religiosity in relation to social change. The current use by the government of "religious fanatics" for counter-insurgency is another source of lessons.

Much depends on the framework and perspective you use. The "modernization" perspective (capitalist industrial development) prescribes different changes from what a revolutionary perspective would. Even within this latter perspective, there is a big difference between those who retain a basically religious worldview and those who advocate a more secular worldview.

8. Does liberation theology also imply that religion need not necessarily be an "opiate," a form of escape? But even in its most radical expression, does not religion retain an idealist and metaphysical view of man and human progress? Is there a possible formula for reconciling the Christian utopia and political-scientific projects of social progress?

That's a lot of questions! I don't think I can answer any one of them adequately. I prefer to approach it, first of all, through praxis. Are there activists, even revolutionary activists, who say that they draw both inspiration and even some theoretical guidance from their religious faith? There are. If so, is their self-consciousness rooted in fact, or is it illusory? Or, more precisely, is there a tendency for their religious consciousness to "wither away" and give way to secular consciousness? Or do they simply undergo a purification of still the same basic religious worldview?

This was part of what I sought to find out when I came back to the Philippines in 1981. I wanted to use my studies in sociology of religion to examine the experience of church people who have involved themselves in the resistance, both overt and covert.

My raw findings revealed two sets of people. One group said that they "outgrew" their religious framework (not only consciousness, but also institution) and assumed an increasingly secular worldview. The other group, which was the bigger one, said that their religious consciousness and praxis underwent purification.

9. Is there an SVD school of thought regarding liberation theology? Fr. Balweg himself has been much quoted regarding his ideas. Is there basis for comparison with, say, the Nicaraguan Jesuits?

No. The activists in the SVD are a minority. There is no comparison with the Nicaraguan Jesuits.

Perhaps most of the older SVD activists do share key experiences and insights, since we worked for quite a number of years with the FFF before martial law. The latest official position of the SVD on justice and peace work is quite progressive, and I'm told that the Philippine delegates had a lot of input into that document. But between official documents and pronouncements and institutional commitment (expressed in assigning personnel and resources plus accepting a certain level of risk), there is still a gap. Most of the "notorious" activists are very marginal to the SVD. I myself had to take a leave of absence in order to avoid jeopardizing the institution's interests in pursuit of my political commitment.

10. When you were released the first time, you went abroad for theological studies. In what particular areas were these studies? Are you working on, or planning to work on your reflections about your life's work?

One study I started but cannot finish, at least not while detained, is the one I mentioned earlier — a sociological study of church people involved in the resistance. This was to have been the first of a two-part study. The second part would be a study of lay Christians, both from the middle class and especially from the peasants and workers. I hope some others who are interested can pick this up.

I have started writing a more systematic reflection on my development as an activist, using the framework of a pre-martial law title: *The Passion, Death and Resurrection of the Petty-Bourgeois Christian*. I hope I can discipline myself enough to finish it.

B. ON PHILIPPINE POLITICS

1. Talk is rife about the post-Marcos era. What are your reflections on this? What is the shape of things to come? How do you size up the party in power and the opposition, both legal and "illegal"?

2. Will the elections of 1986 and 1987 or a possible earlier one, have significance for the Filipino people in terms of social change? Would boycott be a meaningful stand for the people to take? What forms of protest might be suitable in place of a full-blown boycott?

Your questions need a full essay! Anyway, the broader parameters of the post-Marcos political scene will continue to be defined by the US government on the one side, and the revolutionary forces on the other.

Within this framework, any post-Marcos scenario falls into one of two basic categories: either essentially the same coalition of forces in power (the Marcos camp, minus some from its ranks, or plus some from the ranks of the elite opposition), or a new coalition of forces takes over.

There are a lot of possible variation within those two categories. In the first, the key question is whether it will come to power or manage to hold on to power without having recourse to outright military rule. Of course, US support and leverage for one or the other variant would play a major role.

My interest lies, quite naturally, in the alternative coalition that could come to power. This need not be the "democratic coalition government" that is heavily weighted in favor of left forces, at least not in the short term. I tend to agree with those who say that a coalition that includes the left in a minority position could come to power. This can happen only if certain circumstances combine, one of which is that the elections to be held in 1987 or earlier are fairly clean.

From what I can gather, the revolutionary forces are not averse to participating in the coming elections. The so-called "new legal opposition" has the same idea, I guess it would take some really drastic changes in the political scene for these forces to decide on a total boycott of elections.

Of course, I know that short term changes in the composition of whatever coalition holds political power will not, by themselves, solve the fundamental problems of the nation. But

certain short term changes could hasten the advance of the popular movement. It is the maturation of this popular movement and its eventual accession to power that is the surer guarantee that things will really turn around for the majority of our people.

C. ON BEING AN ARTIST

1. You are a poet and a visual artist. What canons, if you can call them that, relating to art and literature, do you live by?

I really have not done much conscious reflection on my praxis as a poet and visual artist. In this sense, I've been more one-sided compared to my politics and theology, where I have always tried to pay attention to both theory and practice.

Poetry and art are just various ways of communicating for me. As in other forms of communication, I try to be as clear as I can to myself about what I want to say, and with whom I want to communicate.

2. The "Ed dela Torre style" is very recognizable and well known. In fact, other artists seem to have copied it. How would you describe this particular style, and do you have any new techniques which you are developing right now?

I find it difficult to describe what you call "Ed dela Torre style." There must be one, since you recognize it. I presume every individual artist develops a distinct style in the course of praxis. But I did not set out to develop a distinct style. I consider myself rather eclectic. Perhaps I am more comfortable with certain forms e.g. what I called a "modified cubism" and also woodcut. Right now, I'm into texture, partly influenced by the rough prison walls, and partly because the act of scratching and gouging and mixing sand and paint releases more pent-up energy and feeling than brushing paint on canvas.

3. What does it take to be a people's artist?

On the one hand, it means being an artist — doing what it takes to be an artist, like honing one's craft, and sharpening one's visions. One does this as a companion of the people as they suffer

and struggle on their long march to liberation. "People" in our present political situation means a cross-class coalition. One must speak to all of them although we can't help but speak more effectively to some rather than others. The concept is not simple. Being with the people and serving the people involves both tactical and strategic considerations. This is true of art, as of politics.

THEOLOGY AS "COMPANION" SPI INTERVIEWS 1985

THE THEOLOGY OF STRUGGLE

SPI: There's talk of "theology of struggle" being developed as the distinct Philippine theology. How do you see your part in this? What elements are most important to you?

ET: As I mentioned in a short article I did for *Kalinangan*, it was Louie Hechanova who proposed the name "theology of struggle." The theology forum I was attending had planned to come up with a book on that theme, and I was to do the sociology of religion part, including a section on Philippine values "From *Pakikisama* to *Pakikibaka.*" I have not been able to follow whatever progress they've made since my arrest. That's more than three years ago!

There's a theological group called THRUST. I don't know enough of their composition and work except the pieces I've read.

I am not comfortable with being called a theologian. I don't have enough written output. Also, I think my theoretical work has

been mainly to help formulate what is called a "political line" for Christians and church people in the struggle, or a "sectoral line."

Whatever can be called a theology of struggle is largely still either oral, rather than written; or mimeographed, rather than printed in books or pamphlets. I am reminded of the process of formation of the biblical books. You had many literary forms e.g. songs, poems, stories, reflection pieces, letters, etc. In this sense, I'm part of the process.

What we need is to enter the stage of compilation and editing. The question is, for what purpose? For what community use? We don't want a book just so we can satisfy our need to tell Christians in other countries that Filipino Christians have a theology, although that is a legitimate desire. It's part of the dialogue and exchange that need to happen among Christians in different situations.

The first purpose must be to serve the current struggle of the people for national liberation and democracy. If we agree on this, I can distinguish three interrelated functions which call for different forms of theology.

The first function is "defensive." Christians in the struggle are subject to all sorts of attack from the powers that be. Among the weapons used against them is the charge that they are not Christian anymore, or that they are on the way to losing their faith, to be replaced by Marxism. Of course this kind of reaction has roots other than theological. But since it also invokes theology, it must also be met on that front. Now, the last thing you should present in your defense is the emerging theology of struggle! That's too new, too strange. What we need is a Gamaliel-type of defense. Someone who is "established," and who can invoke their existing theology against them, so that they do not remain so self-righteous, even though they will continue to look askance at our commitment.

The second function is "purgative." Christians enter into the struggle with whatever theology they've receive from home, church and school. Some of it weighs on them, like excess baggage, preventing them from pursing their pilgrimage at the pace needed.

For example, it took us a while to get rid of the theological identification of faith with a reformist political line. One activist told me he was helped by Cox's *God's World, Man's Responsibility*. A very elementary point, that it is not the church that is the first arena for a Christian, but the world. A special part of this function is "exorcism," or helping Christians see that there are no devils in such scary words (and realities) like struggle, class struggle, armed struggle etc. Not justification; just making them human choices, rather than cosmic conflicts between God and Satan.

What I consider the most challenging is the third function, of theology as "companion." Like a good companion, this theology acknowledges that there are others in the pilgrimage — other ideologies, other words, with their proper roles and spheres of competence. No effort to arrogate to itself everything. On the other hand, like a good companion, it does not hesitate to ask questions and to offer its answers as part of the discussion.

SPI: It's not just a question of theology's function. One essential item is who's going to produce such theology? The grassroots, particularly the BCC's? What about middle-class intellectuals, like you?

ET: Some years back, Abe (Carlos Abesamis) posed this vigorously. He said formally trained theologians are to be technicians serving the grassroot theologians, e.g. through exegetical studies. He has been practicing what he preached.

I remember two reactions to his thesis. One was from the "left." They complained that his view would saddle the grassroots leaders with an additional burden of "theologizing" and delay their political education. The other criticism, was that such insistence on grassroots theologizing did not recognize the need and capacity of middle-class Christians to do theology on the basis of their distinct praxis.

There are at least three factors at play in this question. One is the historical stage of the mass movement's growth. For most of the martial law years, emphasis was on developing the mass movement of the "basic masses" — workers and peasants. Middle class people were seen primarily as assisting that development, rather

than constituting a distinct movement themselves. Now, of course, there's recognition of sectoral movements among middle class people — teachers, nurses, church personnel etc.

The other factor is organizational. Most peasant and worker organizations then had their center of gravity in the underground, due to the repression. The underground was, and continues to be mainly, secular and Marxist in its leadership. The emphasis, naturally, was to develop class consciousness and break down religious barriers. How difficult this is may be seen in the current proliferation of paramilitary organizations that invoke religion even against politically involved BCC's.

The third factor is political, or theoretical. This is also addressed by Marxist intellectuals. On the one hand, there is the truth that "only the masses make history." On the other hand, Lenin's concept of party leadership that introduces theory "from the outside." This means that the fully formulated political line is developed by intellectuals (whether of middle class or working class origins) based not only on the summed-up direct experiences of mass movements, but also on theoretical heritage received from the past.

It's difficult to avoid one of two pitfalls. The first is the "populist" reduction of the intellectual's task to mere gathering and summary of the existing consciousness of the masses. The other is the "dogmatist" arrogance that the masses will have to yield the custody of the correct line to a select group of leaders. How to handle the dialectic between leadership and masses? Between leading, advanced, middle and lower levels of consciousness?

Anyway, the basic insight is correct — it is only when the majority classes consciously carry out any political line that it becomes flesh and blood and makes history. Any theology that would be more than the project of a small group has to meet this same test.

I give a lot of importance to sociological and organizational aspects. For example, in Marxism, the CPP establishes party branches at the grassroots, and gives the same basic party course. But the BCC is looked upon by many church leaders as a threat or only a quasi-church. Realistically, it will be middle class Christians who

have the organization (including underground organization) that will support this theologizing. But it's part anyway of the process, so there's no need to give it less importance.

Think of Solentiname. If we had something like that, it would also be destroyed. We cannot expect the level of struggle arising from the kind of theology produced by the grassroots to remain "safe."

SPI: So far you have been talking of the "theological movement." But what about you? Your own personal process?

ET: You can't really separate personal from community or movement in my case. That's why I still haven't finished the book I set out to write — "The Passion, Death and Resurrection of a Middle Class Christian!"

Anyway, I once wrote that my efforts at theology passed through three stages (I notice I keep talking of three). The first stage was trying to see what God and Christ would look like through Filipino eyes. This meant getting away from the mode of "seeing" that I acquired from Western philosophical thought.

I'm glad I didn't stay there too long. It can be a dead end, and lead to unfair absolute contrasting of Western vs. Eastern (Filipino) way of thinking. The second stage was to look through the eyes of Filipinos who suffer and struggle, and particularly the Filipino peasants. This was more fruitful, though it posed its own set of problems. For example, what sources could I tap? Ileto already discussed this problem in writing history. Oral sources were there, but what sort of generalizations could be drawn?

Finally, the third stage was "through the eyes of Mao." That's a dated expression. The more precise term is "through the eyes of class conscious Filipino proletariat." Clearly, Marxism (including Mao's writings) form part of it. But it is also Filipino, so the incarnation of Marxism in the concrete conditions of the Philippines and the consciousness of the Filipinos is part of it.

This last stage is where the "passion and death" really happens. After all, many writers, both Marxists and Christians, believe that

God and Christ cannot be seen through such eyes. Marxists, because they believe there is nothing to see. Christians, because they believe there is a congenital defect in such eyes.

SPI: Has there been any resurrection? What new face of Christ do you see?

ET: I think I have not gone through the whole passage yet, not all of me, for sure. A resurrected middle class Christian — that I can partly identify with. But what about a proletarian Christian? Is there such an animal, especially if you consider that the organizational expression of a class conscious proletariat is a communist party, and that of a Christian is a church?

That there are Christians in the CPP, I know from the research I did before my arrest. Whether they will remain conscious Christians or become anonymous Christians is an open question. The specific variety of Marxism we have in the Philippines is rooted in the theory and practice of Asian revolutions. No significant participation of revolutionary Christians has had an impact on the theory received by Filipino communists.

In Latin America, Che Guevarra already called for a strategic alliance of Christians and Marxists. He said that the Latin American revolution will be invincible when the Christians discover and live out the revolutionary potential of Christianity.

Here, it took a while for Marxists to consider Christians as more than tactical allies. Now revolutionary Christians are considered strategic allies, in practice. Does this apply also to Christianity? I mean, Christianity not just as an impulse to love and sacrifice, but also in its conceptual and theoretical aspects?

We're nowhere near the position of Marxists and Christians within the FSLN, where they talk not just of strategic alliance, but of unity within the same leading organization.

We have to take our specific characteristics seriously. I can understand the impatience for results, for answers. But if the seed takes time to die and take root, we should not despair that no new

growth will happen. In the fullness of time, "from the blood and ashes of the struggle."

SPI: But surely, there are some glimpses, some hunches? Even if we accept the need for many concepts and theoretical formulations to die or give way, some core gospel remains. Don't you have at least some tentative formulations?

ET: Well, just don't forget they're tentative. When I was still in the seminary, we were told about "kerygmatic theology," or formulating theology so it could be preached. At the same time, I was reading Bonhoeffer, and his question: "How should the gospel be preached to man come of age?" I translated that into: "How should I preach the gospel to Rafael Salas?" I don't know why I thought of him. I guess he symbolized "man come of age," a technocrat whose attitude was that problems exist to be solved by using available resources. No easy recourse to some outside force, *deus ex machina.* No God who came across as filling the gaps could be preached to him, I thought.

Now, I would still think of Salas, but another Salas — Rodolfo, supposedly the chairman of the CPP, if we are to believe the intelligence reports. Also a "man come of age," believing that people can solve their problems collectively, not just within a given society, but even to the point of changing that society. What gospel can be preached to him?

When I was starting out, I thought theology was simply believing that "Christ is the answer," and then listening to the questions people asked, so I could translate that answer in the appropriate language. Now I think the exact opposite. When people ask questions, we should help them look for answers from their own resources, through their own efforts. Many theologians, even of liberation, worry too early about people being too self-reliant and losing a sense of transcendence. I think the main danger our theology poses is still to make people doubt their capacity to find answers to questions. Marx talked of questions being asked only when the conditions for their answers are already present.

Only when people have passed that stage, and when the danger is the opposite — the absolutizing and idolatry that is the temptation of "people come of age," should we preach. No, not Christ as the answer, but Christ as the question.

A second hunch is that religious language will have to take the "*via negativa,*" the process of negation. Remember Thomas Aquinas? After writing all those volumes (which gave me a headache just reading them for my thesis), he was supposed to have said that all he had written were "like straw." Abe said something similar. Sometimes, the best thing to do is to keep silent. But most church leaders (including theologians) get nervous. So they frantically seek another set of words to replace the empty chatter.

Ironically, Marxism could be doing mysticism the necessary service of clearing the mind of all the theological underbrush, the tangle of speculative thought that flourish only outside the unforgiving discipline of materialism and dialectics. Something akin to Zen's "stilling" the body and mind.

Let me give you an example of a "hermeneutic circle" I completed, one of the very few. It's not quite at the level you ask about, but it hints at what you ask for.

When I was starting out as an activist, one of the texts used by religious superiors against our generation was Martha and Mary before Christ. Martha was the busybody, the "activist," but Mary just sat, listening to Christ, the image of the "contemplative." And she was supposed to have chosen the better part.

Those who opposed the social activism we were promoting were by no means contemplatives themselves. Only, they busied themselves in other things, like school work or parish work, etc. So, it was easy to give an *ad hominem* answer. Still, the text bothered me.

Two developments led to a new reading of the text. One was Matthew 25, standard text for activists. Christ identifying himself with the least of our brethren. The other was my shift from doing things for the poor (including lecturing to them about encyclicals) to realizing that I should sit at their feet to learn. Suddenly, Mary

became the image of the mature activist, in solidarity with the people. To see Christ and listen to him. To hear his word and keep it. When did we see you and hear your word?

From that stage, still another cycle. Did Mary just listen passively? Did she not speak also her word? The question coincides with the insight that listening to the people and learning from them involves also addressing our word to them, in response, to provoke further response.

We have to go through that second reading first, before we can do the third.

CHURCH TRANSFORMATION AND SOCIAL TRANSFORMATION

SPI: Politically involved Christians clearly have social transformation, rather than church transformation, on top of their agenda. But you cannot avoid addressing also the latter question, can't you?

ET: In my research, there were even church activists whose initial focus was on church reform, and only later broadened their concern. But it is true that the majority worry about church institutions only within the larger agenda of social change.

I find that Protestants tend to address church transformation as a "normal" item, I guess, because of the Reformation. Catholics concede that "*ecclesia semper reformanda,*" the church needs continuing reform, but it takes greater mental and emotional effort. One of the reasons is that the formal mechanisms of democratic pressure and choice from below (e.g. voting for leaders) is not available for most Catholic institutions. Except for religious superiors, bishops, priests and other church leaders are not subject to election.

The CNL program of 1981 talks of the "national democratic transformation of the churches" as its seventh task, and its special responsibility. What this formulation does is to give the general idea of reform a definite historical shape.

Obviously, this is influenced by the broad direction of over-all social transformation — national liberation and democracy. But it has its internal basis in the theological concepts of incarnation (for nationalism) and church as people (for democracy).

Even at a tactical level, you can't postpone the struggle for church transformation. Otherwise, existing structures and leadership of the churches will prevent or punish its members who involve themselves in social transformation. Also, the churches are a social force, either as an unreformed obstacle or a transformed resource to social change.

I wouldn't settle for a situation where society changes and the churches remain basically the same, tolerated by the new government for tactical purposes, but really not part of the people's effort to build a more humane society.

SPI: I notice that you give a lot of stress to the churches' contribution of personnel and material resources to the struggle. Also, you talk of the national democratic movement recognizing legitimate rights of the churches to property and freedom of worship. But these are categories belonging more to 19th century liberal philosophy. What do you think of the opinion of a Sandinista leader, that the presence of religious in the revolution may contribute to keep the revolution human?

ET: The stress on people and material resources is a corrective to the one-sided preoccupation with the "ideological" contribution of the churches. Both are needed.

Since I was quoting the NDF position, I could refer only to economic and political aspects. But those are the minima. Obviously the realization of the churches about their social involvement will continue. The fact that society will have changed does not make it perfect or static. Like the churches, it's also *semper reformanda*, and the churches are part of the process.

I agree with the Sandinista leader, in the sense that the participation of the greatest number and variety of non-party individuals and organizations makes for greater democracy. It's simple socio-

logy. But I wouldn't interpret that in a "triumphalist" sense, as if Marxists didn't have in them or in their theory what it takes to make a process human. Remember my caution about a "companion theology." We should not claim monopoly of humaneness. Neither should we hesitate to contribute.

SPI: **But isn't there a specifically Christian contribution? It is true that political options are autonomous, and Christians cannot deduce particular options from their faith. Would that make faith merely a private motivation? Is there no contribution in the public sphere?**

ET: **At a sociological level, the question is easier to answer. Presuming that committed Christians act in the public sphere as part of a social institution, then their contribution will be defined by the institution's practice, rather than by a direct unmediated impact of their faith in the public sphere.**

This is not a simple issue, or something we can take lightly. Considering the use of Christianity and church for counterrevolution e.g. Nicaragua, Christians and churches who take sides with the people have more than enough to do!

It is the other level that's harder to answer. I think it is Fely Cariño who poses this repeatedly. He asks if there is not something in Christian theory that can contribute to the vision of an alternative society. I think he is talking not of the utopian element that theologians of liberation propose, or something like the "eschatological reserve" of political theologians. It's not a question of the ultimate counterposing of the Kingdom and the communist vision. No, it's the more concrete agenda of a national democratic Philippines.

I have not done enough thinking on this to give answers, at least not the kind I am ready to fight for.

We should not rush too fast into public functions of faith, at the expense of appreciating its value as personal motivation. With so many risks and costs, including those that result from the weaknesses of companions in the struggle, deep personal motives matter.

At the underground level, Christians are under theoretical pressure because the unifying value is revolutionary commitment. It is to Marxism that revolution is theoretically associated, not to

Christianity. Hence, the whole corpus of Marxist theory, including the various shades of atheism (humanist, scientific, and militant) are more credible. Enough Christians have not been found wanting in commitment and dedication. But they are asked (and also ask themselves) if there are theoretical roots in their faith.

My appreciation of this is closely tied up to the idea of wholeness, a key element of a spirituality for combat. I once had a visitor who asked me how CNL reconciled faith and revolution. I told him stories, rather than a theoretical discourse. I noticed some tears, and asked why he was crying. He said he felt some regret, some loss. At one time he felt he was Christian but wanted to be revolutionary. No one helped him put the two together. So he decided to be revolutionary, leaving behind his understanding of his faith. Later he learned Marxist theory as a CPP candidate member. No, he was not considering a change of identity. He was already comfortable as a Marxist. But he felt he could have been more whole if his Christianity had not been left behind.

I do not say that Christians do not become Marxists except with a sense of loss. No, I have friends who have made that passage and feel more whole, freed from shackles of the mind. All I'm saying is that for many Christians I know, the sense of continuity and identity as Christians in the revolution is no small matter, even if it does not have a specific, public expression.

SPI: **But you yourself say that it is difficult to divorce personal from social. Would it not be difficult to sustain such identity without any community, or organization? That calls for a public aspect.**

ET: **I agree. That's why for Christians who take the risk of joining the underground, organizations like the CNL, are welcome. Like a catacomb church, I guess.**

SPI: **What about Rome? At least for Catholics, traditional attachment to Rome is strong. How do you reconcile a more nationalist and democratic church with the universality and unity of the church, as interpreted by Rome?**

ET: That's a complex and difficult question. Even at a time when Marxism or socialism were not yet part of the picture. Rome did not recognize the Filipino revolutionaries' project of a church, in communion with Rome, but Filipino. This meant excluding all Spanish friars. I don't know if it also meant excluding all other church personnel from non-Spanish countries.

I think William Henry Scott is doing a more comprehensive study of this. I hope he will bring to light the precise theological and political thinking that operated on both sides. But one factor that I consider crucial was the inability of the revolutionary government to stay in power. Once the US colonial government took over, religious nationalism could only suffer a setback, together with the over-all nationalist movement. That had its effect on Rome, also. Rome recognizes power and knows how to adjust to it.

If that lesson is true, then one *conditio sine qua non* for a nationalist Catholic church to remain in communion with Rome because it will get a better hearing from Rome is the coming to power of a nationalist government. Of course there would still need to be effective leadership at both ends. Part of my concern is to take care of our end. Rome's end? Well, the recent efforts to "normalize" relations with the Patriotic Church in China might be more than realpolitik. I hope it's a sign of a new awareness of alternative forms of communion between Rome and local, national churches.

The Vatican's perception of relations between the Catholic church and revolutionary regimes is unfortunately based on the historical experience of little or no church participation in the process of revolution, followed by mutual suspicion. If the church is tolerated, its base is seen as people not committed to the revolutionary project, or worse, hostile to it.

I had initial hopes that the Nicaraguan experience would give the Vatican new reason to think of a different relationship, in the same way that it has given Marxists fresh impulse to incorporate into their thinking the phenomenon of consciously Christian par-

ticipation in a revolution. I still hope, but events keep battering my hope.

My first impulse is to contest your premise of strong traditional attachment to Rome among Filipino Catholics. But I recall what happened when Pope Paul VI visited the Philippines in 1970. I was with Khi Rho activists in the barrios of the Laguna lakeshore area. We were urging them to organize against possible eviction should the coastal road being planned by the Laguna Lake Development Authority push through. It was a frustrating effort. Most of the people said they would fight only when they saw the bulldozers. One of them even asked if we were communists. I asked, with some hurt, why he did not believe we were Christians. "You are from the city. There's no money for you in what you're doing. Only communists do that," he explained. "Besides, if you are Christians, why are you not in Manila to meet the Pope? "

APPENDIX

REFERENCES

1. To Be a Priest, Here and Now. Sermon at First Mass (December, 1968) *Here and Now* 1(1969).

2. Some Notes for A Theology of Social Reform. *Philippine Priests Forum (PPF),* 1.3 (September 1969).

3. The Role of the Priest in Social Reform. Speech at the First National Convention, Philippine Priests Inc., *PPF* (September, 1970).

4. The Challenge of Maoism and the Filipino Christian. *Challenges for the Filipino*, ed. R.J. Bonoan (Ateneo, Manila 1971).

5. Christians in the Struggle for National Liberation. *Salvation Today*, Leadership Manual (Manila, 1977).

6. The Passion, Death and Resurrection of the Petty-Bourgeois Christian. *Asia-Philippines LEADER.* (March 1972).

7. Church and Liberation in the Philippines. Speech at the Third National Convention, Philippine Priests Inc., *PPF* (June 1972)

8. A Monument for the Dead, A Movement for the Living. *PPF* (March 1972).

9. The Gift of Final Perseverance. Message to Fr. Nilo Valerio (Sept. 16, 1985). *SIMBAYAN,* 4,3 (October 1985).

10. "To Hunger and Thirst for Justice" Poems and Letters from Camp Olivas. *PINTIG 1* (1979).

11. "Theology is like Poetry" Letter from Bicutan. *PINTIG 1* (1979).

12. Prose and Poetry from Bago Bantay. *PINTIG 2* (1985).

13. My Five Years in Prison. *Office of Human Development (OHD)* Papers (1980).

14. A Theology of Struggle. *KALINANGAN* (September 1983).

15. It's a Very Poor Christianity That Cannot Handle Struggles." *Breakthrough* (May 1980).

16. Of Churches and Politics. *Philippine News and Features PNF* (January 1985).

FOOTNOTES

The Challenge of Maoism and the Filipino Christian

1. Mao Tse Tung, *Selected Works* (Peking: Foreign Language Press, 1969). Roman and arabic numerals here and in succeeding quotations from Mao indicate, respectively, volume and page numbers of the *Selected Works.*

2. Amado Guerrero, *Philippine Society and Revolution* (Manila: Pulang Tala Publications, 1970), p. 2.

3. *Ang Bayan,* 1 (1969), p. 1.

4. This quotation from Mao's speech "Reform in Learning, the Party, and Literature" delivered at the opening of the Party School in Yenan on February 1, 1942 has been edited and 'purified' in the *Selected Works.* English translation of the unedited version is from Stuart Schram. *The Political Thought of Mao Tse Tung* (Great Britain: Penguin Books, 1969), p. 174.

5. Mao Tse Tung, *On the New Stage* (A Report to the Sixth Plenum of the Sixth Central Committee, October 1938), Chapter 7, *Selected Works II,* 209 gives a 'purified' version.

6. *Constitution of the Communist Party of the Philippines 1969,* "Preamble". This is a document found in Capas, Tarlac.

7. Translation in Schram, *op. cit.,* pp. 427-428.

8. *Ibid.,* pp. 297-298.

9. Guerrero, *op. cit.,* pp. 3-4.

10. *Peking Review,* no. 15 (10 June 1958), p. 6.

11. Martin Kenner and James Petras (eds.), *Fidel Castro Speaks* (New York: Grove Press, 1969), p. 278.

12. Courtesy of *Breakthrough,* Student Christian Movement.

13. "Gospel and Revolution" [Manifesto by 16 Bishops of the Third World]. *New Blackfriars* (December, 1967), pp. 140-148.